TOP 10
CAPE TOWN
AND THE WINELANDS

Top 10 Cape Town and the Winelands Highlights

The Top 10 of Everything

CONTENTS

Cape Town and the Winelands Area by Area

Streetsmart

Within each Top 10 list in this book, no hierarchy of quality or popularity is implied. All 10 are, in the editor's opinion, of roughly equal merit.

Title page, front cover and spine
Thelema Mountain, as seen from a vineyard in Stellenbosch
Back cover, clockwise from top left *Colourful huts on Muizenberg beach; Table Mountain; Western Cape; a vineyard in Stellenbosch; City Hall*

The rapid rate at which the world is changing is constantly keeping the DK Eyewitness team on our toes. While we've worked hard to ensure that this edition of Cape Town and the Winelands is accurate and up-to-date, we know that opening hours alter, standards shift, prices fluctuate, places close and new ones pop up in their stead. So, if you notice we've got something wrong or left something out, we want to hear about it. Please get in touch at **travelguides@dk.com**

Welcome to
Cape Town and the Winelands

Modern visitors would surely agree with Sir Francis Drake's description of the region as "the fairest Cape in the whole circumference of the earth". Perched at the foot of Africa, Cape Town's golden beaches, wild forests and rugged peaks melt into rolling, vine-covered slopes. With DK Eyewitness Top 10 Cape Town and the Winelands, it's yours to explore.

Cape Town is a haven for outdoor enthusiasts: you can hike the footpaths on **Table Mountain**, picnic on the lawns at **Kirstenbosch**, don a wetsuit and learn to surf or people-watch at a pavement café over a glass of local wine. Within an hour's drive there are hundreds of wine estates, where you can sample vintages in centuries-old manor houses or bold modern buildings decked out with local art.

Food and drink are just as important as natural beauty in the so-called Mother City, whether you're looking for Cape Malay *bobotie* and a syrupy *koeksister* in **Bo-Kaap** or fine dining and a flight of wines at a **Stellenbosch** estate. Festivals are also a way of life here, epitomized by the flamboyant **Cape Town Carnival** and the colourful **Kaapse Klopse** New Year parade.

Whether you're coming for a weekend or a week, our Top 10 guide brings together the best of everything that Cape Town and the Winelands have to offer, from the cafés, shops and museums of the **V&A Waterfront** to the windswept coves of the **Cape of Good Hope**. The guide has useful tips throughout, from seeking out what's free to finding the best beaches, plus six easy-to-follow itineraries designed to tie together a clutch of sights in a short space of time. Add inspiring photography and detailed maps, and you've got the essential pocket-sized travel companion. **Enjoy the book, and enjoy Cape Town and the Winelands**.

Clockwise from top: **View of the Lion's Head from Table Mountain, African penguin on Boulders Beach, V&A Waterfront in Cape Town, wine estate near Franschhoek, a protea, the national flower, at Kirstenbosch National Botanical Garden, beach huts at Muizenberg, guards during the Key Ceremony at the Castle of Good Hope**

Exploring Cape Town and the Winelands

Cape Town and its glorious surrounds offer something for every type of traveller, from the hardy hiker to the discerning gourmet. However long your stay, you'll want to make the most of your time, so here are two sightseeing itineraries to help you get the very best out of your visit to Cape Town and the Winelands.

Robben Island

See Cape Town map, right

Clifton

Camps Bay

Kirstenbosch National Botanical Garden

Groot Constantia

Buitenverwachting

Hout Bay

Chapman's Peak Drive

Muizenberg

Kalk Bay

Simon's Town

Cape of Good Hope

Cape Point

Table Mountain's Upper Cableway viewpoint offers breathtaking vistas.

Two Days in Cape Town

Day ❶
MORNING
Take the cable car to the top of **Table Mountain** (see pp22–3) and allow an hour or so to admire the views.
AFTERNOON
Wander the **Company's Garden** (see pp12–13) and visit the fascinating Iziko Slave Lodge. Drop in to the poignant **District Six Museum** (see pp18–19) and end your day with an afternoon tea at the **Belmond Mount Nelson Hotel** (see p114).

Day ❷
MORNING
Get an early start for the drive to **Cape Point** (see pp32–3) and have breakfast at the **Two Oceans Restaurant** (see p89). Then take the scenic drive to **Simon's Town** (see pp30–31) to see the colony of African penguins.

AFTERNOON
Enjoy lunch and wine tasting at the historic **Groot Constantia** (see pp28–9). Complete your day with a stroll through the **Kirstenbosch National Botanical Garden** (see pp26–7) and high tea in the Tea Room Restaurant.

Seven Days in Cape Town and the Winelands

Day ❶
Start with a trip to the top of **Table Mountain** (see pp22–3). Later, have lunch on trendy Bree Street, haggle for curios at **Greenmarket Square** (see p67) and follow the Fan Walk to **Green Point Urban Park** (see p70).

Day ❷
Book ahead for the boat trip to **Robben Island** (see pp16–17) and take a fascinating guided tour.

Key
— Two-day itinerary
— Seven-day itinerary

Cape Town

from Robben Island
V&A Waterfront
BOAT
Green Point Urban Park
Two Oceans Aquarium
Bree Street
Greenmarket Square
Iziko Slave Lodge
Castle of Good Hope
Company's Garden
District Six Museum
Belmond Mount Nelson Hotel
Table Mountain

0 kilometres 10
0 miles 10

0 km 1
0 miles 1

and explore the park's many museums. Reward yourself with a decadent high tea at the **Belmond Mount Nelson Hotel** (see p114).

Day 5
Drive out to **Stellen-bosch** (see pp34–5) to indulge in some wine tasting at gorgeous Lanzerac or family-friendly **Spier** (see p57). Book ahead for lunch at one of the estates. Sip wine (unless you are the driver) under the trees at **Boschendal** (see p92), then make your way to pretty **Franschhoek** (see pp36–7) and spend the rest of the day and evening exploring the galleries and restaurants of the main street.

Day 6
Enjoy a French-themed breakfast in Franschhoek, then head to **Paarl** (see p92) and visit Spice Route to taste artisanal produce. Afterwards, head back to Cape Town to spend some time enjoying the beautiful beaches of **Camps Bay** and **Clifton** (see p51).

Day 7
Try a surfing class in **Muizenberg** (see p50) or browse the eclectic shops of **Kalk Bay** (see p87). Head to the Constantia wineries for lunch, and visit **Groot Constantia** (see pp28–9) or **Buitenverwachting** (see p80) for a little wine tasting. Then take a stroll or hike through **Kirstenbosch National Botanical Garden** (see pp26–7).

Enjoy a seafood lunch at the **V&A Waterfront** (see pp14–15) followed by a visit to the aquarium, a bit of shopping and watching street performers.

Day 3
Head to **Hout Bay** (see p86) for breakfast, ideally on a weekend when the market is operating. Follow stunning **Chapman's Peak Drive** (see p86) then explore the windswept **Cape of Good Hope** (see pp32–3). Pay an afternoon visit to the delightful penguin colony at Boulders Beach and then dine at the water's edge in **Simon's Town** (see pp30–31).

Day 4
Explore the **Castle of Good Hope** (see pp20–21), South Africa's oldest build-ing, then brush up on more recent history at the **District Six Museum** (see pp18–19). Enjoy a picnic in the **Company's Garden** (see pp12–13),

Stellenbosch is the lovely historic capital of the lush Winelands.

Top 10 Cape Town and the Winelands Highlights

View from Cape Point, overlooking
the Cape of Good Hope

TOP 10 Cape Town and the Winelands Highlights

Cape Town, set between the imperious heights of Table Mountain and the blue depths of the Atlantic, offers a Mediterranean climate, a vibrant Afro-fusion cultural scene, a rich sense of history and fine colonial architecture. Beyond it lie the Cape Peninsula, magnificent beaches and, of course, the lush Winelands to explore.

0 km 5
0 miles

Century City Goodw
M14
Cape Town
see inset map Milnerton
N1 R102 Pa
Clifton Pinelands
Table M3 N2
Mountain **5**
M6 **6** Kirstenbosch National
Botanical Garden
Constantia
Groot Constantia
Wine Estate **7** Bergvliet
Chapman's
Point
Noordhoek M4 Muizenberg
M65 Fish Hoek
Kommetjie M6 Glencairn
8 Simon's Town and
Boulders Beach
Table
Mountain
National
Park
Cape of
Good Hope
9

1 Company's Garden
This park was established by the first Dutch settlers in 1652 and is bordered by an eclectic mix of museums and galleries *(see pp12–13)*.

2 V&A Waterfront and Robben Island
Enjoy cafés, shops and bars at this waterfront complex. It is also the departure point for trips to Robben Island *(see pp14–17)*.

3 District Six Museum
This stirring Cape Town museum documents the apartheid-era evictions of "non-whites" from the central suburb of District Six to the remote Cape Flats *(see pp18–19)*.

WHITE ARTISANS
REST ROOM & TOILET
BLANKE AMBAGSMANS
RUSKAMER EN TOILET.

4 Castle of Good Hope
Constructed in the 1660s and 1670s, South Africa's oldest extant building houses two museums. The ramparts overlook the Grand Parade, where crowds gathered to greet Nelson Mandela on his release from jail in 1990 *(see pp20–21)*.

5 Table Mountain
The thrilling aerial ascent of magnificent Table Mountain leads to a succession of stunning views over the Cape Peninsula and the Winelands *(see pp22–3)*.

6 Kirstenbosch National Botanical Garden

At its best during the spring wild-flower season, this garden preserves and propagates rare indigenous plant species and is a year-round visitor attraction *(see pp26–7)*.

Groot Constantia Wine Estate 7

South Africa's oldest estate, Groot Constantia is noted for its old-world Cape Dutch architecture nestled amongst leafy vineyards *(see pp28–9)*.

8 Simon's Town and Boulders Beach

With an abundance of quaint Victorian façades overlooking the splendid False Bay, this sleepy naval town is famed for the colony of adorable African penguins that waddles around on nearby Boulders Beach *(see pp30–31)*.

Cape of Good Hope 9

Pink-hued proteas, grazing antelope and mischievous baboons can be observed at the peninsula's southern tip, where a clifftop light-house offers spectacular bird's-eye views over Cape Point *(see pp32–3)*.

Stellenbosch 10

Despite its wealth of impressive Cape Dutch architecture, South Africa's second-oldest town is better known – and justifiably so – as the most central base for exploring the renowned Winelands *(see pp34–5)*.

⭐ Company's Garden

This peaceful oasis at the heart of Cape Town, with stunning views of Table Mountain, is set amid the city's most important concentration of old buildings and museums. It was established by Jan van Riebeeck in 1652 to provide fresh produce to passing Dutch ships. By the 18th century, it had been transformed into a world-renowned botanical garden and exported bulbs and other produce to Europe.

1 Parliament Buildings and Tuynhuys

On the southeast side are the Neo-Classical parliament buildings and the Tuynhuys **(above)**, the president's official Cape Town residence.

2 Rose Garden

The site of the Cape's first wine-producing vine and a source of rose-water in the Dutch era, this garden **(below)** contains many rose varieties, set out in a radial pattern.

Company's Garden

3 The Company's Garden Restaurant

With tables outside, as well as a choice of nest-like treehouses and swinging chairs, the restaurant is perfect for a light lunch or a good cup of coffee.

④ Aviary and Slave Bell

The aviary opposite The Company's Garden Restaurant houses many indigenous birds. The so-called Slave Bell is actually a fire bell from Greenmarket Square.

⑥ Iziko Slave Lodge

Founded in 1679, this handsome building, once an unsanitary and cramped home for enslaved people, is now a museum charting the history of the slave trade.

⑦ Iziko South African Museum and Planetarium

This fine 19th-century mansion displays natural history, rock art and artifacts. Beside it stands the planetarium.

ARCHBISHOP DESMOND TUTU

Desmond Tutu (b.1931), the first Black Archbishop of Cape Town, was the bishop of St George's Cathedral. During his tenure, the church was a key centre of the anti-apartheid movement. Post-apartheid, this 1984 Nobel Peace Prize winner chaired the Truth and Reconciliation Commission (1995–2002).

⑧ St George's Cathedral

This Anglican cathedral (right) was a centre of political protest during the 1980s. The oldest part of the building is a crypt designed by Sir Herbert Baker.

⑤ VOC Vegetable Garden

Inspired by the layout of the historical vegetable garden, this tribute to the park's original purpose highlights the need for urban food gardens.

⑨ Iziko South African National Gallery

From an initial bequest of 45 paintings in 1871, this gallery is now one of the country's leading art museums. Along with African and European collections, it has temporary shows.

⑩ Delville Wood Memorial

With sculptures by Alfred Turner, this memorial (below) was designed by Herbert Baker and was unveiled in 1930 to commemorate the many South African casualties of World War I at Delville Wood, France.

NEED TO KNOW

MAP P5 ▪ Entrances on Queen Victoria St and Adderley St ▪ www.iziko.org.za

The Company's Garden Restaurant: 021 423 2919; open 8am–5pm daily; www.thecompanysgarden.com

Iziko South African Museum and Planetarium: open 9am–5pm daily;

museum: adm R30 (adults), R15 (kids 6–18 yrs), under 5s free; planetarium: adm R60 (adults), R30 (kids under 19)

Iziko Slave Lodge: open 9am–5pm Mon–Sat; adm R30 (adults), R15 (kids 6–18 yrs), under 5s free

Iziko South African National Gallery: open 9am–5pm daily; adm R30 (adults), R15 (kids 6–18 yrs), under 5s free

TOP 10 ⭐ V&A Waterfront

Set between the majestic Table Mountain and the sparkling waters of the Atlantic, the V&A Waterfront is integral to modern-day Cape Town, and reconnects the city to the sea. The complex opened in 1992 and has played a key role in reversing the economic decline that had gripped the old docklands since the 1960s. A working harbour to this day, the V&A Waterfront is South Africa's most-visited tourist destination, with a huge choice of eateries, shops, sights and leisure activities, including tours to Robben Island.

1 Two Oceans Aquarium
Highlights here **(above)** include Rockhopper and African penguins, the kelp forest and the predator exhibit. Try to visit at feeding times.

2 Cape Wheel
An iconic landmark, this 40-m (130-ft) observation wheel **(right)** has 30 air-conditioned cabins and offers a four-revolution ride lasting between 12 to 15 minutes.

3 Alfred Mall
Lined with alfresco bars and cafés, this converted Edwardian warehouse is an excellent spot to down refreshments while soaking up the idyllic views over the harbour to Table Mountain.

4 Harbour and Bay Cruises
You can take harbour tours, seal-watching trips and sunset cruises in Table Bay with one of the boat operators found on Quay 5.

5 Swing Bridge and Clock Tower
A piece of ornate Victoriana, the iconic Clock Tower **(right)** dates back to 1882. It is reached via a modern swing bridge that opens to accommodate passing boats.

HISTORY OF THE DOCKLANDS

The docklands started to take shape in the 19th century, when Prince Alfred (son of Queen Victoria) began the construction of the Alfred Basin by tipping a load of stones into the sea in 1860. Despite extensive development over the years, several Victorian buildings at the waterfront, such as the Ferryman and Mitchell's Pubs and Breakwater Lodge, are still standing.

NEED TO KNOW

MAP P2, Q1–2 ■ Information Centre, Dock Rd ■ www.waterfront.co.za

Shops: open 9am–9pm daily

Cape Wheel: 021 418 2502; open 10am–9pm Sun–Thu, 9am–10pm Fri, Sat & public holidays; adm R155 (adults), R80 (kids 4–17 yrs); www.capewheel.co.za

Two Oceans Aquarium: 021 418 3823; open 9:30am–6pm daily; adm R210 (adults), R160 (kids 14–17 yrs), R100 (kids 4–13 yrs); www.aquarium.co.za

Zeitz MOCAA: Silo District; 087 350 4777; open 10am–6pm Thu–Sun; adm R210 (adults); www.zeitzmocaa.museum

■ There are many bars, restaurants and cafés to choose from *(see p76)*.

V&A Waterfront

6 Zeitz MOCAA
Set in a historic grain silo, Zeitz Museum of Contemporary Art Africa is the world's largest museum dedicated to 21st century art from Africa and its diaspora. The striking building also houses The Silo Hotel.

7 Victoria Wharf Shopping Mall
Shop till you drop or dine at one of the many restaurants, then catch a movie at the Art Nouveau or Nu Metro cinemas – all in one of South Africa's largest malls.

8 Nobel Square
Life-sized statues of four Nobel Peace Prize winners – Albert Luthuli, Desmond Tutu, F W de Klerk and Nelson Mandela – are set alongside Noria Mabasa's intriguing Makonde-style sculpture.

9 Nelson Mandela Gateway
This is the embarkation point for day tours to Robben Island. It also displays photographs and information documenting the island's history.

10 The Watershed
Over 150 stalls in South Africa's largest indoor craft market **(above)** offer everything from African beadwork to tarot readings and holistic health treatments.

TOP 10 ⭐ Robben Island

Robben Island, in Table Bay, is South Africa's version of Alcatraz and has been a place of exile since Van Riebeeck's day. Its first political prisoner, a Khoekhoe interpreter trader named Autshumatom, was sent here in 1658. By the 1760s, the island held 70 prisoners. It is best known for its role under apartheid, when Nelson Mandela, Walter Sisulu, Govan Mbeki (father of Thabo Mbeki) and Jacob Zuma among others were held here. The last prisoner left in 1996, and the island is now a museum.

Maximum 1 Security Block

With tours sometimes run by former political prisoners, this block (right) is the highlight of any visit to the island. Tours include a peek into Mandela's cell and a look at photos of that era.

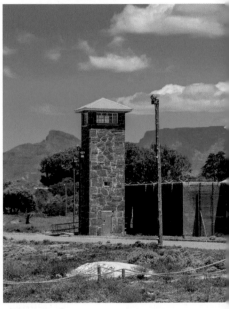

2 Murray's Bay Harbour

Robben Island's small harbour is host to a large breeding colony of African penguins (above). The island hosts about 132 bird species, including a large number of African black oystercatchers.

3 Jan van Riebeeck Quarry

The blue slate used as paving in the building of the Castle of Good Hope was quarried by Van Riebeeck at the far south of the island. The quarry closed in 1963.

4 Robben Island Village

Formerly home to prison wardens, this village comprises residential quarters for the museum staff. It also has two old churches, the Church of the Good Shepherd, built in 1895, and the Garrison Church, dating back to 1841.

5 Leper's Graveyard

This cemetery (left), seen from the bus tour, is testament to the island's role as a leper colony from 1846 to 1930.

6 Lighthouse
Not open to visitors, the lighthouse **(left)** was built in 1864 on Minto Hill, the island's highest point. It replaced the fire beacons that were once in use.

7 Ferry Trip
The 30-minute ferry trip from the V&A Waterfront is best on calm, clear days, which provide fabulous views across Table Bay. Keep a look out for dolphins and seals.

8 Kramat of Tuan Guru
The island tour includes a stop at the shrine of Tuan Guru, an Indonesian Islamic cleric who was jailed here by the Dutch in the 18th century.

9 Robert Sobukwe Complex
A depressing sight, this is where anti-apartheid activist Robert Sobukwe was held in solitary confinement in 1963–9.

10 Limestone Quarry
Mandela and other prisoners undertook hard labour here. In 1990, former prisoners built a cairn **(right)**.

NELSON MANDELA

Mandela, born in 1918, was the first member of his family to attend school. His political career began in 1944, when, along with Oliver Tambo and Walter Sisulu, he formed the African National Congress Youth League. Mandela was accused of high treason in 1956, but the charges were dropped after a four-year trial. However, he was captured and incarcerated on Robben Island in 1964 under charges of treason. Released from jail in 1990, he went on to win the Nobel Peace Prize in 1993 and became president of South Africa in 1994. He stepped down in 1999, and died in 2013.

Robben Island

NEED TO KNOW

MAP A2 ■ Departures from the Nelson Mandela Gateway at the V&A Waterfront ■ 021 413 4200 ■ www.robben-island.org.za

Boats at 9am, 11am, 1pm, 3pm weather permitting; guided tours with return ferry ride: 3½–4 hours

Adm R600 (adults), R310 (kids under 18)

■ Book in advance online and arrive 30 minutes prior to the scheduled departure time of the boat.

■ There are no dining facilities on the island, but refreshments are for sale at the small curio shop.

TOP 10 ⭐ District Six Museum

Founded in 1994, this award-winning community museum draws on a rich repository of artifacts and recollections supplied by the forcibly dispossessed residents of District Six. They celebrate everyday life as it was in a once-vibrant multicultural suburb that was re-zoned as a whites-only area under the Group Areas Act during the apartheid era. Possibly the most moving of Cape Town's many museums, it provides some insight into the insidious effects of the racial discrimination propagated by the government on ordinary people.

1 Little Wonder Store

It might be small, but this bookshop **(above)** on the ground floor stocks a comprehensive selection of titles about District Six and the many other mass evictions undertaken by the apartheid regime.

2 Methodist Church

The Buitenkant Methodist Church, left standing after most of District Six was razed to the ground in 1966, became a place of contemplation for former residents and was chosen as the site for the museum in 1994.

3 Barbershop Display

This cheerfully nostalgic exhibit is a reconstruction of a typical 1950s' District Six barbershop, complete with period advertising plates pinned to the wall.

4 Nomvuyo's Room

This exhibit **(right)** re-creates the single room that was home to the author Nomvuyo Ngcelwane, her parents and three siblings before their eviction.

5 Bloemhof Flats Display

These poignant displays show photographs of Bloemhof Flats, a multiple-block housing development that was built over slummy Wells Square and famed for its football team.

THE DESTRUCTION OF DISTRICT SIX

Cape Town's sixth municipal district was established in 1867. Its residents were people who were freed from slavery, immigrants, and people of mixed race. The forced removal of Black residents by the police began in 1901; by 1967, 60,000 residents had been removed to the Cape Flats. The first to return post-apartheid were handed their house keys by Mandela.

"Formation, Resistance, Restitution" Wall Panels

6

Using a combination of pictures, hard facts and interviews with former residents, this series of three wall panels (right) recounts the history of District Six since its creation in 1867.

District Six Museum

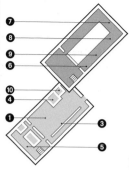

Key to Floorplan

▢ Ground floor
▢ First floor

Painted Floor Map

7

In the main hall (above), a hand-painted street map of District Six before its demise is annotated by former residents with the locations of their houses before the bulldozers arrived.

NEED TO KNOW

MAP Q5 ▪ 25A Buitenkant St ▪ 021 466 7200 ▪ www.district six.co.za

Open 9am–4pm Mon–Fri

Adm R45 (self-guided tours), R60 (hourly guided tours), R20 (kids under 16)

▪ Many guided township tours start with a peek into District Six Museum, but it is also worth visiting independently to absorb the poignant exhibits.

▪ The District Six Museum Café serves coffee, light snacks, local sweets, such as *koeksisters*, and Cape Malay-inspired lunches, including *bobotie*, tomato *bredie* and spicy chicken curry.

Sound Domes

8

Place your shoes on the marked footprint in front of the mural on the inside front wall of the first floor, and listen to a sequence of ten different stories narrated by former residents of District Six.

Tribute to Langarm Pioneers

9

Grainy photographs, period recordings and a stack of 78s rpm discs by swing musicians form a tantalizing introduction to the distinctively South African Langarm "jazz" music that rocked District Six during the 1930s, 1940s and 1950s.

The Story of Horstley Street

10

The memorial hall charts the history of Horstley Street. The mosaic and concrete floor includes extracts from written recollections of its residents.

TOP 10 ⭐ Castle of Good Hope

Constructed between 1666 and 1679, the imposing Castle of Good Hope is the oldest functional building in South Africa. It was built with slate quarried on Robben Island and sandstone from Lion's Head, a small mountain between Table Mountain and Signal Hill. Originally located alongside Table Bay to protect the new Dutch settlement from naval invasion, its seaward wall now stands about 1 km (half a mile) inland after land reclamation. Following an extensive program of restoration that took place during 1969–93, it now houses two permanent museums and hosts occasional temporary exhibitions.

1 Governor's and Secunde Houses
Part of the 12-m- (39-ft-) high inner wall that bisects the courtyard, the Governor's and Secunde's houses were built by Simon van der Stel in the 1690s to accommodate himself and his *secunde* (second-in-command).

2 Main Entrance
Built in 1683 the main entrance is notable for its bell tower **(below)** made of imported yellow *ystelsteen* and sculpted masonry depicting a lion with seven arrows to represent the provinces of The Netherlands. The key ceremony, which symbolizes the ceremonial unlocking of the castle, is held here on weekdays.

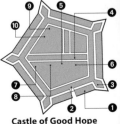

3 Kat Balcony
This elegant and ornate balcony **(above)** has an Anton Anreith bas-relief sculpture. During Dutch colonial times, it was the ceremonial site for greeting visitors and for the reading out of judicial sentences.

Castle of Good Hope

4 William Fehr Collection
This collection, donated by Dr William Fehr includes paintings by Thomas Baines. Other works give insight into the lives of early settlers.

5 "Fired" Ceramics

This exhibition **(left)** features a rare collection of African pottery, with one of the renowned "Lydenburg Heads" dating to around AD 500.

6 Inner Archway and Old Well

The inner archway is flanked by the covered well that once provided water to castle residents, and has a memorial to the dead of World War I.

7 Block B

The castle's oldest section, to the right of the main entrance, dates from the 1660s. A staircase leads to the grassy bastion, offering fine views out across the Grand Parade.

8 Dungeon and Torture Chamber

This room was the site where prisoners were tortured, in accordance with the Dutch law that required a confession before sentencing.

CITY HALL

Cape Town had no city hall prior to 1905, when the foundation was laid in front of the Grand Parade opposite the castle. The Italian Renaissance-style building houses an opulent interior with marble staircases and a stained-glass window commemorating King Edward VII. On his release from jail, Mandela made his first public speech from its balcony.

9 Military Museum

The Cape's military past, from the first clash between Bartolomeu Dias *(see p40)* and the locals in 1488 to the 1899–1902 South African War, is documented here **(left)**.

10 Leeuhek and Moat

Visitors can gain entrance to the castle by crossing its moat **(above)**. On the way is the Leeuhek (Lion's Gate), a sentry portal, which was built in 1720 and is crowned with two lion sculptures.

NEED TO KNOW

MAP Q5 ■ Corner of Strand & Darling Sts ■ 021 787 1249 ■ www. castleofgoodhope.co.za

Open 9am–5pm daily; free guided tours at 11am, noon, 2, 3 & 4pm daily (except 25 Dec & 1 Jan)

Adm R50 (adults), R25 (kids 5–18 yrs), under 4s free

■ If you visit on a weekday, aim to be at the main gate at 10am or noon, first for the key ceremony and then for the firing of the signal cannon.

■ Situated inside the castle to the left of the main entrance gate, Re5 Restaurant *(open 9am–4pm daily)* serves inexpensive deli-style snacks and light meals that have a Cape Malay influence. There is outdoor seating under the colonnades.

🔟 ⭐ Table Mountain

South Africa's most celebrated geographical landmark, Table Mountain dominates the Cape Town skyline from almost every direction. This remarkably flat (hence the name) sandstone plateau is sometimes swathed in the cloudy shroud that locals refer to as the "tablecloth". Most people reach the top using the cableway that opened in 1929 and has since taken over 27 million passengers to the summit. The main attraction of the summit is the fabulous views, which capture Cape Town and the Peninsula in their full glory.

2 Abseil Africa
A must for the adventurous traveller is Abseil Africa's 112-m (367-ft) abseil route (see p53) down the ledge of Table Mountain overlooking Camps Bay.

3 Platteklip Gorge Trail
This demanding but popular alternative to the cableway runs from Maclear's Beacon to Tafelberg Road.

1 Cableway
Travel in a small circular cable car (above), complete with rotating floor and 360° views of Cape Town and Table Bay. The incredible 5-minute ride to the top seems too short, and comes within inches of the sheer cliff face below the Upper Cableway Station.

4 Dassies and Other Animals
Look for the rock hyrax, or dassie, a guinea pig lookalike often seen basking on the plateau. Other wildlife includes klipspringer and southern rock agama lizard.

5 Upper Cableway Viewpoint
Emerge from the Upper Cableway Station for a view of Signal Hill, Robben Island in Table Bay and the Hottentots Holland on the eastern horizon.

TIPS FOR WALKERS

Table Mountain has several well-marked trails to the summit, and these are graded according to difficulty. Hikers must wear proper walking boots and are advised to check with the Lower Cableway Station before setting out, as weather conditions may change without warning. Hiking on windy or misty days is not recommended.

Table Mountain viewed from Robben Island

6 Fynbos Vegetation

A sweeping glance over Table Mountain's sandstone plateau might be your first exposure to *fynbos*, a heath-like cover **(above)** with muted shades offset by fiery pink proteas, multicoloured disas and spectral silver trees.

8 Maclear's Beacon

The highest point on Table Mountain **(left)** is marked by an 1865 cairn. It is an attractive goal for peak-baggers and ramblers, and there's some great scenery along the way, too.

7 Dassie, Agama and Klipspringer Trails

These three circular, paved paths, although not teeming with wildlife, offer glorious views and are wheelchair friendly. Dassie is the shortest.

9 Birdlife

The *fynbos* attracts nectar-dependent sunbirds and sugarbirds. The redwing starling and chat often visit the summit. Look out for swifts, kestrels and black eagles.

10 Sign 15 Viewpoint

This viewpoint offers sweeping vistas over the mountainous spine of the Cape Peninsula, with glimpses of Simon's Town and Kommetjie through the hills.

NEED TO KNOW

MAP H1 ■ Tafelberg Rd ■ 021 424 8181 ■ www. tablemountain.net

Cable cars leave every 10–15 minutes from 8:30am–5pm in mid-winter and 8am–8:30pm in midsummer; free, guided 30-min walks hourly, 9am–3pm daily

Fare R200 one-way or R380 return (adults), R100 one-way or R190 return (kids 4–17 yrs)

■ Book tickets online to avoid the queues.

■ The cableway is inoperable on days when mist and cloud settles on the mountain, so try to visit when the weather is good.

■ The Table Mountain Café, with its gourmet self-service deli, caters to all tastes.

TOP 10 ⭐ Kirstenbosch National Botanical Garden

One of the world's great botanical gardens, Kirstenbosch was established in 1913 to protect the immense floral wealth of the Western Cape. Set on the eastern slopes of Table Mountain, the lower sections of the garden are planted with lush indigenous flora, blending into a natural cover of *fynbos* and forest at higher altitudes, accessible by a network of footpaths.

Sunbird on a protea plant

Fynbos Walk ①
This footpath passes through colourful *fynbos* vegetation **(right)** unique to the Cape. The colourful proteas found here bloom in winter and spring, when they attract the long-tailed Cape sugarbird.

② Visitors' Centre
Located at the main entrance (Gate 1), the centre sells a good map of the garden. There's also a gift shop **(above)**, a café and a bookshop that sells books about South Africa's flora and fauna.

③ Mathews Rockery
A labyrinthine collection of dry-country plants, including some massive euphorbia trees, this is most stunning in winter, when aloe blooms attract nectar-feeding sunbirds.

④ Tree Canopy Walkway
Opened to mark the garden's centenary, this walkway snakes along among the tree tops of the arboretum, giving magnificent views of Table Mountain.

⑤ Conservatory
The glass-topped conservatory **(left)** boasts several plants from arid southern African habitats. At the centre, a spectacular baobab, typical of the arid Kalahari, rises above other species.

Previous pages Upper Cableway Station atop Table Mountain

Sculpture Garden 6

Situated in the eastern corner of Kirstenbosch, the sprawling Sculpture Garden is scattered with superb examples of contemporary stone sculptures **(right)**, created by artists in Zimbabwe's Shona tradition. Some are available for purchase.

8 Van Riebeeck's Hedge

This thick hedge of native wild almonds, planted by Jan van Riebeeck in 1660, marked the boundary of the new Cape Colony. The almond-like fruit of this plant is poisonous.

9 Useful Plants Garden

Complete with well-marked signs, this garden **(below)** has a selection of medical plants used to treat everything from headaches to secondary symptoms of HIV/AIDS.

WILDLIFE IN THE GARDENS

Though best known for its plants, Kirstenbosch also supports varied fauna, and is home to 200 vertebrate species. The birds include the Cape sugarbird, the lesser double-collared sunbird, the steppe buzzard that breeds on Table Mountain and the Cape francolins that haunt the streams. Mammals include grey mongooses, rock hyraxes, Angulate tortoises and three frog species that are indigenous to the region.

10 Vlei

A wooden boardwalk crosses the small reed-lined *vlei* (marsh), which is a magnet for a wide variety of birds as well as other wildlife, such as the Cape porcupine, grysbok and mongoose, although they can be difficult to spot.

7 Cycad Garden and the Dell

This section of the garden has large trees, a stream and a pool set below a natural amphitheatre with cycads that evolved 150–200 million years ago.

NEED TO KNOW

MAP H2 ■ Rhodes Drive, Newlands ■ 021 799 8783 ■ www.sanbi.org/gardens/kirstenbosch

Open Apr–Aug: 8am–6pm daily; Sep–Mar: 8am–7pm daily

Adm R200 (adults), R27 (kids and scholars), under 6s free

Conservatory: open 9am–5pm daily

■ Botany enthusiasts should time their visit to coincide with one of the free guided walks *(Mon–Sat; see website for times)*.

■ Sunday Summer Sunset Concerts *(see p63)* are held from November to April.

■ Moyo Restaurant *(www.moyo.co.za)* serves African specialities, and the Kirstenbosch Tea Room *(www.fynkos.co.za)* offers light snacks.

TOP 10 ⭐ Groot Constantia Wine Estate

Founded in 1685 by Simon van der Stel, Groot Constantia is the oldest wine-producing farm in South Africa. It boasts a wonderful setting below the Constantiaberg on the Cape Peninsula, and is situated about 10 km (6 miles) south of central Cape Town. Home to some of the country's most interesting Cape Dutch architecture, it features two gabled buildings completed under the late-18th-century proprietorship of Hendrik Cloete. It was under the Cloete family, who owned the farm from 1778 to 1885, that Constantia's dessert wines won international acclaim, and the estate became the official supplier to Napoleon Bonaparte, exiled on St Helena. Bought by the Cape Government in 1885, it has been a non-profit company since 1993.

Historic Gardens ③

Dotted with trees, some of which were planted in van der Stel's day, the estate gardens **(right)** are delightfully peaceful and make the ideal spot for a leisurely stroll. They afford lovely views of the vineyards and the sandstone Constantiaberg mountain range.

① Jonkershuis

Expanded from an outbuilding, the thatched Jonkershuis (meaning the house of the eldest son or *jonkheer*) is an attractive Cape Dutch building with a fine restaurant **(above)**.

② Orientation Centre

The orientation centre is a useful first port of call, with its scale model of the estate and informative panels discussing the long history of the Constantia Estate.

④ Coach House Museum

The Isaacs Transport Collection is displayed in a courtyard behind the Jonkershuis. Exhibits include old coaches, carts, bicycles, and vintage mule and ox wagons.

NEED TO KNOW

MAP H2 ■ Groot Constantia Rd ■ 021 794 5128 ■ www.groot constantia.co.za

Open 10am–5pm daily

Wine tasting: adm R100; cellar tours: adm R115 (tasting included); chocolate and wine pairing: R150

Iziko Homestead Museum: 021 795 5149; open 10am–5pm daily; adm R30 (adults), R15 (kids 6–18 yrs); www.iziko.org.za

■ The estate's restaurants stay open for dinner.

■ Most visitors just stop by for the museums and the wines, but the entire estate is worth exploring.

7 Cloete Cellar

A long, narrow structure dating from 1791, the building has South Africa's famous triangular gable and a striking Rococo pediment sculpted by Anton Anreith. Originally used as a wine cellar, it now houses displays of antique wine storage and drinking vessels **(left)**.

SIMON VAN DER STEL

Simon van der Stel was the first non-European and also the first person born of mixed parentage to be appointed the Governor of the Cape. He was born on a ship in Mauritius, where his father, Adrian, had been posted by the United Dutch East India Company. His mother, Monica Van Goa, was the daughter of an enslaved woman. Van der Stel played a key role in the foundation of Stellenbosch and Simon's Town, both named after him.

8 Historic Gates and Main Drive

The magnificent main drive leads right up to the main complex, passing through a gate **(above)** that dates from the 18th century.

10 Wine-Tasting Cellar

Just inside the entrance gate, the wine-tasting and sales centre offers excellent wines for visitors to sample and buy. One of them, the highly praised Grand Constance, revives the historic dessert wine tradition that earned the estate its fame.

5 Historic Bath

This ornate oval pool, located on the Constantiaberg slopes, is of uncertain origin, but it is similar in style to the gable of the main house, which dates from the late 18th century.

6 Manor House Façade

Expanding on van der Stel's house, Hendrik Cloete later added the front gables and commissioned the sculpture by Anton Anreith in the niche.

9 Iziko Homestead Museum

This museum in the manor house is decorated in a style typical of an 18th-century estate owner **(above)**. The old Cape furniture and art were donated by collector Alfred de Pass in 1927.

TOP10 ⭐ Simon's Town and Boulders Beach

Simon's Town is named after the first Cape Colony Governor Simon van der Stel, who selected its harbour as a safe winter alternative to Table Bay. With a 144-year tenure as Britain's main regional naval base, prior to the South African navy taking over in 1957, it is lent a distinct character by its wealth of Victorian architecture and lovely location on steep slopes above a string of sandy beaches. Most famous of these is Boulders Beach, with its African penguins.

1 Boulders Beach
The sheltering rocks after which Boulders **(above)** is named make it a lovely, secluded spot for a swim, and, if you're lucky, you might find yourself taking a paddle with a penguin *(see p46)*.

2 South African Naval Museum
Set in a masthouse and sail loft from the 1740s, this museum features a life-size replica ship's bridge, complete with simulated rocking motion.

3 Jubilee Square and Quay
Overlooking the harbour are Jubilee Square and Quayside Mall **(below)**. Boat trips launch from the jetty to explore False Bay and Seal Island.

4 Historic Mile
The concentration of venerable buildings in Simon's Town is at its most dense along the so-called Historic Mile – a succession of Victorian façades that run down St George's Street **(above)**. Stop by the bar at the Lord Nelson Hotel, built in 1929.

5 Willis Walk
Situated outside the national park, this wheelchair-friendly boardwalk **(left)** offers opportunities to spot penguins and their offspring, and *fynbos* birds such as Cape canaries and martins.

6 Foxy Beach
You'll see several hundred penguins here surfing or strutting on the sandy beach. Before heading along the boardwalks to view the birds, brush up your penguin knowledge at the handy Boulders Visitor Centre.

7 Seaforth Beach
Sheltered by rocks and occasionally visited by penguins from nearby Boulders, Seaforth offers safe swimming in calm weather. Its popular beachfront restaurant is a welcome retreat when the wind gets too strong.

BOULDERS BEACH ORIENTATION

Boulders lies to the south of Simon's Town and is accessed from the main road to Cape Point. Foxy and Boulders Beaches lie within an annexe of Table Mountain National Park and are entered via two separate gates. The Boulders Visitor Centre is at the Foxy Beach gate. Willis Walk, which connects the two gates, is outside the park and is open at all times.

8 Metrorail Southern Line
The Metrorail service **(above)** that begins in Cape Town is one of the world's great suburban train rides, offering breathtaking views on its way to Simon's Town's Victorian railway station.

9 Kayaking
For an alternative view of the coast and its penguins, hire a kayak at Simon's Town harbour for a 2-hour guided paddling trip to Boulders Beach and back.

10 Simon's Town Museum
Built as a Governor's Residence, this museum houses an exhibition on apartheid's forced removals and a more lighthearted display about a naval dog.

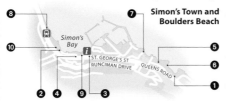

Simon's Town and Boulders Beach

NEED TO KNOW

MAP H4 ■ Simon's Town Visitor Centre ■ 111 St George's St ■ 021 786 8440 ■ www.simonstown.com

Boulders Visitor Centre/ Penguin Colony: open Feb–Mar & Oct–Nov: 8am–6:30pm daily (Apr–Sep: to 5pm), Dec–Jan: 7am–7:30pm daily; adm R170 (adults), R85 (kids); www.sanparks.org

Metrorail Southern Line: www.metrorail.co.za

Kayaking: Kayak Cape Town; adm R350; www.kayakcapetown.co.za

Simon's Town Museum: Court Rd; open 10am–4pm Mon–Fri, 10am–1pm Sat; adm R10; www.simonstownmuseum.org.za

■ Dine at the Seaforth Restaurant *(see p89)* or on the pier at Bertha's *(www.berthas.co.za).*

TOP 10 ⭐ Cape of Good Hope

Though Cape Point is not the southernmost point in Africa, most visitors walk away with the distinct sensation that they've seen the end of the continent – such is the scenic drama of the storm-battered headland, whose precipitous cliffs rise to 250 m (820 ft) from the vast blue sea. The Cape of Good Hope (part of Table Mountain National Park) is also of interest for its wealth of fauna. It has a cover of pastel-hued *fynbos*, with more plant species than are indigenous to the entire British Isles.

1 Rooikrans
Just 1 km (half a mile) from the main road to Cape Point, this superb viewpoint (**above**) is the best spot for seasonal whale watching. A footpath leads to the rocky beach below.

2 Gifkommetjie Circular Drive
This road loop leads through subtly shaded fields of *fynbos* to a ridge studded with mushroom-like, balancing rock formations. The views are stunning, and energetic visitors can follow the little-used 3-hour walking trail to *Hoek van Bobbejaan* (Baboon's Corner). Look out for wild tortoises.

3 Cape Point Ostrich Farm
At this private ostrich breeding farm (**right**) you can get close to the world's largest bird. Guided tours explain the full life cycle of an ostrich. There is also a reptile rehabilitation centre here.

NEED TO KNOW
MAP H6

Table Mountain National Park: 021 780 9010; open Apr–Sep: 7am–5pm, Oct–Mar: 6am–6pm; adm R340 (adults), R170 (kids 2–11 yrs); www.capepoint.co.za

Cape Point Ostrich Farm: 021 780 9294; open 9:30am–5:30pm daily; half-hourly tours R100 (adults), R50 (kids 6–16 yrs); www.capepoint ostrichfarm.com

Funicular: return trip R80 (adults), R35 (kids 2–11 yrs)

■ Wild Chacma baboons are common here. They can be aggressive if you are carrying food.

■ By the car park, the Two Oceans Restaurant serves meals during the day.

6 Climb/ Funicular to Cape Point

The final ascent to spectacular Cape Point involves hiking a steep footpath, or taking the funicular **(left)** – a rope-supported railway car designed to cope with such gradients.

7 Buffelsfontein Visitor Centre

This pretty Cape Dutch farmhouse should be your first stop if you plan to explore the area. Apart from a stock of books and leaflets about the reserve, it also houses a natural history museum.

FALSE BAY WHALES

Between July and November, the whales that pass through False Bay can be observed from the southernmost part of Table Mountain National Park. Good vantage points are Rooikrans and other beaches along the eastern seaboard as well as the Lighthouse Keeper's Trail, behind the upper funicular station. The most common is the southern right whale, which can reach a length of around 15 m (49 ft). Bryde's whales, humpback whales and orcas can also be spotted.

4 Buffels Bay

This sandy, surf-washed arc is a great place for a picnic lunch – there are even *braai* (barbecue) facilities available, though keep an eye out for baboons. There's also a tidal pool for safe swimming.

5 Kanonkop Walk

A short walking trail that starts at Buffelsfontein, Kanonkop Walk leads to the old signal cannon after which it is named. It passes a 19th-century lime kiln and offers some splendid views across False Bay. Look out for the blue disa that flowers here in January and February.

8 Bordjiesdrif

The tidal pools are good for marine life, and the artificial rock pool above the beach is safe to swim in. Sights here include a cross in honour of Vasco da Gama's landing in 1497, and the igneous Black Rock.

9 Cape Point Lighthouse

Built between 1913 and 1919 using rocks carried by hand from the present-day car park, this is South Africa's brightest lighthouse **(right)**. It stands at 238 m (781 ft) above sea level on the highest section of Cape Point's rocky peak.

10 Cape of Good Hope Footpath

The 90-minute return trail **(above)**, from the car park to the Cape of Good Hope beach below, offers magnificent views of the lighthouse and an opportunity to detour to the gorgeous Diaz Beach.

TOP 10 ★ Stellenbosch

The second oldest town in South Africa, Stellenbosch has a scenic location on the banks of the Eerste River below the Jonkershoek Mountains. It was founded by Simon van der Stel in 1679 and has been a centre of viticulture for centuries. Today a university town, its stately avenues are lined with a contemporary array of restaurants, cafés, bars and shops, offset by the historic Cape Dutch buildings and the shady trees that earned it the nickname of Eikestad (Town of Oaks). The short drive to nearby Franschhoek via the Helshoogte Pass is packed with must-see sights.

4 Dorp Street

The best-preserved road in Stellenbosch, Dorp Street is lined with pre-20th-century Cape Dutch buildings. The finest façades (right) are between the junctions of Herte and Drostdy streets.

1 Botanical Garden

The leafy Botanical Garden (above), founded by the University of Stellenbosch in 1922, is famous for its collections of *fynbos* plants, ferns, orchids and bonsai trees, and for its dry-country succulents from Namibia.

5 Lanzerac Wine Estate

This is the closest wine estate to Stellenbosch. First planted with vines in 1692, it was then known as Schoongezicht (beautiful view). Its excellent wines and a fine restaurant make it worth a detour.

2 Jan Marais Nature Reserve

Founded in 1919, the reserve protects indigenous *fynbos* and small wildlife. Highlights include a labyrinth and a pond.

Stellenbosch

2 200 m (215 yards)
5 2 km (1 mile)

3 Village Museum

Each of this museum's four charming period-furnished houses (right) represents phases in the town's development; the most recent one dates from the 1830s.

Oom Samie Se Winkel 6

Named after former owner Oom (Uncle) Samie Volsteedt, this landmark trading post (see p94) stocks homemade sweets, traditional handicrafts and Africana (right).

7 The Braak

The village green (braak) is enclosed by historic buildings, notably the Anglican, thatch-roofed Church of St Mary (1852) with its combined Neo-Gothic and Cape Dutch influences, and the Rhenish Church (1823), with a Baroque pulpit.

8 Toy and Miniature Museum

Housed in a Rhenish parsonage, this museum has tiny houses, antique dolls and other nostagic toys, plus a perfectly re-created Blue Train, which travels from a miniature Stellenbosch to Matjiesfontein.

UNIVERSITY OF STELLENBOSCH

South Africa's premier Afrikaans university started life in 1866 as the Stellenbosch Gymnasium, set in a building that still stands on Dorp Street. The university alumni include four of South Africa's prime ministers (Jan Smuts, D F Malan, J B M Hertzog and H F Verwoerd) and anti-apartheid activists such as Beyers Naudé and Heinrich Grosskopf.

9 Rupert Museum

To the town's southwest, this museum of South African art shows works by artists such as Irma Stern and Walter Battiss.

10 Moederkerk

Opposite the Village Museum, on the site of the original Dutch Reformed Church that burned down in 1710, is the Moederkerk (Mother Church), a tall Neo-Gothic building (below) with a steeple that was completed in 1866.

NEED TO KNOW

MAP D2 ■ Visitor Information Centre ■ 47 Church St ■ 021 886 4310 ■ www. visitstellenbosch.org

Botanical Garden: Cnr Neethling & Van Riebeeck Sts; open 8am–5pm daily; adm R15; www.sun.ac.za

Jan Marais Nature Reserve: Marais Rd; 021 808 8188; open 8am–6pm daily

Village Museum: 37 Ryneveld St; 021 887 2937; open 9am–5pm Mon–Sat (to 1pm Sun); adm R50 (adults), R20 (kids 2–17 yrs); www.stelmus.co.za

Lanzerac Wine Estate: 1 Lanzerac Rd; 021 887 1132; tasting daily, see website for details; adm R75; www.lanzerac.co.za

Toy and Miniature Museum: Market St; 021 882 8861; open 9am–4pm Mon–Fri (to 2pm Sat); adm R15 (adults), R5 (kids 2–17 yrs); www.stelmus.co.za

Rupert Museum: Stellentia Ave; 021 888 3344; open 10am–5pm Mon–Fri, (till 4pm Sat & Sun); www. rupertmuseum.org

■ For details of restaurants in Stellenbosch, see p98.

Stellenbosch to Franschhoek

Boschendal wine estate, between the Drakenstein and Simonsberg ranges

1 Boschendal
MAP E2 ■ Pniel Rd, Groot Drakenstein ■ 021 870 4516/7 (tasting); 021 870 4273/4 (picnic reservation) ■ Tasting 10am–6pm daily; cellar tours: 1:30pm & 3pm daily; tasting fee ■ www.boschendal.com

At the gateway to the Franschhoek Valley, Boschendal offers wine-tasting and picnic baskets for a decadent lunch.

2 Pniel
MAP E2

Founded by the Berlin Mission Society in 1834 to house people freed from slavery, Pniel remained zoned for Black people during apartheid, despite its location. A 19th-century church and the 1992 Freedom Monument marking the emancipation of enslaved people are landmarks.

3 Franschhoek Motor Museum
MAP F2 ■ R45 towards Franschhoek ■ 021 874 9002 ■ Open 10am–5pm Mon–Fri, 10am–4pm Sat–Sun ■ Adm ■ www.fmm.co.za

Motor Museum racing car

In the prestigious L'Ormarins Estate, this museum is a magnet for car enthusiasts. The collection of over 220 rare vehicles includes an 1898 Beeston motor tricycle and a 2003 Ferrari Enzo.

4 Delaire Graff and Tokara Wine Estates
Delaire Graff: MAP E2; Helshoogte Rd; 021 885 8160; tasting 10am–5:30pm daily; tasting fee; www.delaire.co.za ■ Tokara: MAP E2; Helshoogte Rd; 021 808 5900; tasting 10am–5pm daily; tasting fee; www.tokara.co.za

These estates, perched on the rim of Helshoogte Pass, are perfect for a late lunch. Visitors can enjoy superb views over the Winelands over a glass of the local bubbly.

THE HUGUENOTS

This group was formed of Protestants who fled France to escape Catholic persecution under Louis XIV. Franschhoek is a legacy to their influx to the Cape in 1688. Due partly to an edict that Dutch should be the sole language of education, local government and commerce, the Huguenots swiftly integrated into the established culture. They were major contributors to South Africa's emergence as a top wine producer. Many Afrikaans surnames are of French origin – some, such as De Villiers, have survived, while others have adapted, such as Cronjé (Cronier) and Nel (Neél).

⑤ Mont Rochelle
MAP F2 ■ Dassenberg Rd ■ 021 876 2770 ■ Tasting 10am–6pm daily; tasting fee ■ www.virginlimited edition.com/en/mont-rochelle

A 5-minute drive – or a steep half-hour walk – from Franschhoek, this small wine estate boasts lovely thatched Cape Dutch buildings. It offers a great view over the Franschhoek Valley and Middagkrans Mountains, best enjoyed from the two fine restaurants here.

⑥ La Motte
There's plenty to see and do at this estate *(see p96)*. Join a tutored themed wine tasting, or simply sample their award-winning reds, whites and bubbly under your own steam. Take a guided walk around the extensive grounds, nose around the fascinating museum and then visit the Pierneef à La Motte restaurant *(see p99)* for lunch or afternoon tea.

La Motte's elegant restaurant

⑦ Huguenot Monument
MAP F2 ■ Lambrechts Rd ■ Open 9am–5pm daily ■ Adm

This stone monument, built on the outskirts of Franschhoek in 1938–48, commemorates the arrival of the

Symbolic Huguenot Monument

Huguenots in 1688. The three high arches represent the holy trinity, while a statue of a woman on a globe displays various religious symbols.

⑧ Hillcrest Berry Orchards
MAP E2 ■ 021 885 1629 ■ Helshoogte Pass Rd ■ Open 9am–5pm daily ■ www.hillcrestberries.co.za

Hillcrest, about 10 km (6 miles) from Stellenbosch, cultivates seven types of berries. Its confections can be tasted at the restaurant or bought at the gift shop.

⑨ Dutch Reformed Church
MAP F2 ■ Huguenot Rd

Franschhoek's architectural gem, the Dutch Reformed Church, was built in 1848. Set below the surrounding mountains, the church's whitewashed gables and 19th-century bell tower make a pretty, pastoral picture.

⑩ Huguenot Memorial Museum
MAP F2 ■ Lambrechts Rd ■ 021 876 2532 ■ Open 9am–5pm Mon–Sat, 2–5pm Sun ■ Adm ■ www.museum.co.za

This excellent museum documents the daily life of the French settlers who gave Franschhoek its name. There is a fine collection of old Bibles, including one printed in 1636.

The Winelands

The Top 10 of Everything

A colony of African penguins waddling across the sands at Boulders Beach

🔟 Moments in History

① Prehistory

The earliest signs of human habitation along Table Bay date back 1.4 million years and consist of Stone Age tools of the Acheulean culture. San hunter-gatherers arrived around 30,000 years ago and left a legacy of rock-art sites, notably in the Cederberg Mountains north of Cape Town. Khoekhoe pastoralists first arrived with their fat-tailed sheep around 2,000 years ago.

② The Portuguese Arrive

In 1488, Portuguese navigator Bartolomeu Dias became the first European to round the Cape. This led to a succession of clashes with the Khoekhoe that culminated in Captain d'Almeida's death in Table Bay in 1510.

Statue of Bartolomeu Dias

③ Foundation of Cape Town

In 1652, Jan van Riebeeck, an employee of the Dutch East India Company (VOC), founded a victual station in Table Bay to provide fresh produce to passing VOC ships. Within a century, Cape Town was home to settlers from Europe, though enslaved people outnumbered free citizens.

④ British Occupation and the Great Trek

The governance of Cape Town by the British in 1795 led to the emancipation of enslaved people in 1834. This angered slave-owning Boers (Dutch farmers), who in the Great Trek of 1836–43 moved north and founded Boer Republics, notably the Free State and Transvaal.

⑤ South African War and Unionization

The South African War of 1899–1902 was initiated by English imperialists to gain control of the Johannesburg goldfields. This bloody three-year engagement led to the formation of the Union of South Africa in 1910, which comprised the Cape, Natal, Transvaal and the Free State. Former Boer general Louis Botha became the first prime minister.

⑥ Foundation of Apartheid

After the National Party (NP) was voted in by the electorate in 1948, parliamentary acts formalized racial inequities into the ideological monolith apartheid ("separateness").

Painting of the Dutch Cape Colony at the Cape of Good Hope

7 Sharpeville Massacre and Rivonia Trial

Resistance to apartheid was galvanized by the police massacre of 69 civilians at a peaceful protest at Sharpeville in 1960. This led to the formation of Umkhonto we Sizwe – the armed wing of the banned African National Congress (ANC) – under Nelson Mandela, who was convicted of treason with other anti-apartheid leaders in the Rivonia Trial of 1962–3.

8 Foundation of the UDF

In 1983, more than 15,000 anti-apartheid activists congregated at Mitchells Plain to form the United Democratic Front (UDF), effectively the domestic representative of the ANC in apartheid's dying years.

Nelson Mandela's release

9 Release of Nelson Mandela

President F W de Klerk lifted the ban on the ANC in February 1990, and Mandela was released from prison after 27 years. He made his first public speech after his imprisonment outside Cape Town's City Hall (see p21).

10 Democracy

In May 1994, the ANC swept to victory in South Africa's first fully democratic elections, after securing eight of the nine provinces, the exception being the Western Cape, the last stronghold of the NP. Mandela was inaugurated as president.

TOP 10 FAMOUS SOUTH AFRICANS

Archbishop Desmond Tutu

1 Nelson Mandela
South Africa's most famous son (see p17) was incarcerated in prisons around Cape Town for 27 years.

2 Archbishop Desmond Tutu
This Nobel Peace Prize winner (see p13) served as Anglican Archbishop of Cape Town between 1985 and 1995.

3 Miriam Makeba
Best known for her 1967 hit single "Pata Pata", Mama Africa, was named a UN Goodwill ambassador in 1999.

4 Winnie Madikizela-Mandela
The "Mother of the Nation" was repeatedly imprisoned and placed under house arrest by the apartheid regime. She later served as the leader of the ANC Women's League.

5 J M Coetzee
Booker Prize winner and recipient of the 2003 Nobel Prize for Literature.

6 Steve Biko
This anti-apartheid activist and founder of the Black Consciousness Movement died in police custody in 1977.

7 Brenda Fassie
The "Madonna of the Townships" was a popular recording artist prior to her drug-related death in 2004.

8 Elon Musk
Born and raised in Pretoria, Elon Musk is the co-founder of Tesla and became the world's richest person in 2021.

9 Charlize Theron
The winner of the best actress Oscar for her role in Monster in 2004.

10 Trevor Noah
An award-winning comedian, Trevor Noah honed his craft in South Africa. He is the host of The Daily Show.

🔟 Local Culture

Apartheid exhibits in the District Six Museum

1 District Six Museum

This museum *(see pp18–19)* is a testament to the iniquitous Group Areas Act passed by the National Party in the 1950s and 1960s. The museum focuses on day-to-day life in District Six before apartheid's bulldozers rumbled in.

2 Langa
MAP H1

Founded in 1927, the oldest Black township in Cape Town was an integral part of the resistance to apartheid for the resident Xhosa people. Walking tours of Langa include the Gugu S'Thebe Arts Theatre and the middle-class area known as "Beverley Hills".

Mosaic in the Langa township

3 Iziko Slave Lodge

This building opposite the Company's Garden was founded in 1679 as quarters for the immigrants – the force behind the Cape's agricultural economy – imported from Malaysia and Indian Ocean islands. Now a museum *(see p13)*, it charts the history of the slave trade through a series of multimedia displays.

4 Rock Art Gallery, Iziko South African Museum
MAP P5 ▪ 25 Queen Victoria St ▪ 021 481 3800 ▪ Open 9am–5pm daily ▪ Adm ▪ www.iziko.org.za

South Africa is one of the world's most important repositories of rock art, with several sites dating back 10,000 years scattered through the country. This gallery has a superb display, including re-creations and an original panel relocated here.

5 Gugulethu
MAP H2

Although this up-and-coming township retains the reputation of a crime hotspot, it is safe to visit during the day with a guide. It is home to a *braai* (barbecue) restaurant, Mzoli's, where you can buy meat from the butcher and then take it to be grilled.

6 Robben Island
A trip to Robben Island (see pp16–17) takes you on a tour of the island's historical sites. It finishes at the maximum security prison where anti-apartheid activists were incarcerated, and includes a viewing of Nelson Mandela's cell.

7 Khayelitsha
MAP C3
An isiXhosa phrase meaning "Our New Home", Khayelitsha, on the Cape Flats, started life in the 1950s after the Group Areas Act was passed. It is best visited as part of a township day tour.

8 Long Street
Affordable restaurants, trendy shops and a smattering of LGBTQ+ friendly nightspots line Long Street (see p72), one of the liveliest and most integrated parts of the city. It is the hub of the city's backpacker scene.

Quirky shops and cafés on Long Street

9 Bo-Kaap Museum
MAP P4 ■ 71 Wale St, Bo-Kaap
■ 021 481 3938 ■ Open 9am–5pm Mon–Sat ■ Adm ■ www.iziko.org.za
This museum explores the evolution of the Bo-Kaap – an Islamic suburb that has been inhabited by the Cape Malay people since the abolition of slavery in the 1830s.

10 Imizamo Yethu Township
This recent township (see p85) is set on the slopes above Hout Bay. Despite the tough living conditions, the atmosphere is welcoming. Tours are provided by the residents.

TOP 10 SLANG WORDS AND PHRASES

Lekkers, or sweets (candies)

1 Lekker
Good or nice (as in "we had a lekker time"). It can also mean that something is tasty. Sweets (candies) are called *lekkers* in Afrikaans.

2 Ag!
Pronounced "Ach", and meaning "Oh man", this can be an expression of distaste (ag, sis!), sympathy (ag, shame!) or annoyance (ag, no!).

3 Bru
Derived from the Afrikaans *broer* (brother), this is a generic term of male address, a bit like "dude" in the USA or "mate" in the UK.

4 Eish!
This isiXhosa interjection might be used like the English "whew", as in "Eish! That was a crazy day".

5 Babalas
A Cape Coloured (see p68) term for a hangover.

6 Just Now
This phrase, which frequently confuses and amuses visitors to Cape Town, means "a bit later" – or "much later"!

7 Now Now
This expression of urgency means that something will happen much sooner than "just now". It does not, however, mean "now".

8 Izit?
Literally "is it", this is often interjected when another person speaks. It is similar to the English "really?"

9 Yebo
This word is often used by all language groups to signal agreement.

10 Jol
The word means party or any good time, and is used both as a noun ("where's the jol?") or a verb ("let's jol").

Parks and Reserves

1 Jonkershoek and Assegaaibosch Nature Reserves

A ramblers' paradise, these adjoining reserves (see pp90–91) protect the Jonkershoek Mountains, which rise 1,526 m (5,005 ft) on the eastern outskirts of Stellenbosch. Apart from the wildlife and montane *fynbos*, they also offer day walks, ranging from a stroll through the Assegaaibosch wildflower garden, to the challenging 18-km (11-mile) Swartboskloof Trail.

2 Cederberg Wilderness Area

About a 3-hour drive north of Cape Town, the rugged Cederberg (see p102) is a dream for hikers, rock climbers, mountain bikers, photographers and stargazers. Day hikes visit marvellous russet-coloured sandstone rock formations, and there are some well-equipped camp sites and cottages for overnight stays.

Rocky outcrops at Cederberg

3 Harold Porter National Botanical Garden

This botanical garden (see p104) in Betty's Bay is an excellent place to see *fynbos* flora, including the *Disa uniflora* in its natural habitat, proteas, ericas and restios. The birdlife found in the garden is an added attraction for avid bird-watchers, with most *fynbos* endemics well represented.

Pelicans at Table Bay Nature Reserve

4 Table Bay Nature Reserve

MAP B2 ■ Grey Ave, Table View
■ 021 444 0315 ■ Open 7:30am–5pm daily ■ Adm ■ www.friendsof rietvlei.co.za

Located in Milnerton and Table View, the Rietvlei section of this reserve is one of Cape Town's top bird-watching sites. It protects the Diep River floodplain, which attracts freshwater and marine birds. Almost 200 species have been recorded to date. Between October and March, there is an influx of migrant waders.

5 Silvermine

MAP H3 ■ 021 789 2457
■ Open May–Aug: 8am–5pm; Sep–Apr: 7am–6pm ■ Adm
■ www.sanparks.org

Part of the central section of Table Mountain National Park, Silvermine is a refreshing alternative to the Table Mountain massif. The Silvermine River Walk provides an introduction to *fynbos* vegetation and birdlife, while the steeper walk to Noordhoek Peak and Elephant's Eye Cave offers spectacular oceanic views.

6 Kogelberg Biosphere Reserve

Just 100 km (62 miles) from Cape Town, the craggy mountains of the Kogelberg feel like true wilderness. Book an eco-friendly cabin well in advance or visit the reserve (see p104) to kayak the river, hike mountain trails and spot the wild horses.

7 West Coast National Park

Centred on the sheltered Langebaan Lagoon, this marine park *(see p101)* is popular with bird and watersport enthusiasts. Apart from the coastal scenery, attractions include wildlife such as eland, bontebok and springbok. Visit in August and September, when the blooming wild flowers in the Postberg section are a magnificent sight.

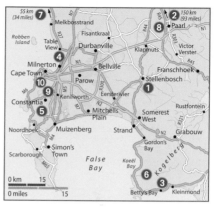

8 Paarl Mountain Nature Reserve

MAP E1 ■ Jan Phillips Mountain Dr, Paarl ■ 021 807 6231 ■ Open Apr–Sep: 7am–6pm daily; Oct–Mar: 7am–7pm daily ■ Adm

Situated on the outskirts of Paarl, with a mix of montane *fynbos* and indigenous forests, this reserve protects the granite domes, which give the town its name. This reserve is a great place for a bracing walk, and is also popular with anglers and mountain bikers.

9 Kirstenbosch National Botanical Garden

On the eastern slopes of Table Mountain, these landscaped gardens *(see pp26–7)* showcase South Africa's peerless indigenous plant varieties, and can be explored on a network of well-maintained, mostly wheelchair-friendly footpaths.

10 Table Mountain National Park

MAP T4 ■ 021 712 0527 ■ Opening hrs vary for each section ■ Adm for select sections ■ www.sanparks.org

Proclaimed as a national park in 1998, this urban park extends from Signal Hill in the north to Cape Point at the tip of the Cape Peninsula *(see pp32–3)*. This rich biodiversity, with an estimated 2,200 plant species and fauna ranging from Chacma baboons and rock hyraxes (dassies) to endemic birds and frogs, thrives within metropolitan Cape Town.

Hikers in Table Mountain National Park

🔟 Wildlife Experiences

Pelicans at Rondevlei Bird Sanctuary

1 Bird-watching, False Bay Nature Reserve - Rondevlei Bird Sanctuary

This large wetland on the Cape Flats is easily the best place to spot waterbirds in suburban Cape Town. Among the 230 species recorded here are the great white pelican, African spoonbill and various herons *(see p85)*.

2 Harbour Cruise

City Sightseeing Harbour Cruise: departs from Two Oceans Aquarium, Dock Rd; 021 511 6000; open daily (see website for times); www.citysight seeing.co.za ▪ Waterfront Charters: departs from Quay 5; 021 418 3168; open 9am–5pm daily; www.water frontcharters.co.za

Operators on the V&A Waterfront offer cruises through the harbour with a near certainty of sighting Cape fur seals, gulls and terns.

On longer cruises out to Table Bay you might also catch sight of dolphins or whales.

3 Penguin Colony, Boulders Beach

Waddling around like tipsy tuxedoed waiters, these flightless birds are a firm fixture on the tourist itinerary. The 2,000-strong colony at Boulders Beach *(see p30)* was founded by two breeding pairs in 1982.

4 Scuba Diving and Snorkelling

The kelp forests and tidal pools of the Atlantic offer excellent opportunities for diving *(see p52)* to glimpse weird and wonderful marine creatures.

5 Land-Based Whale Watching

Peak season: Jun–Nov; calving season: Jul–Aug

The Western Cape has the world's best land-based whale watching. Cliffs at Hermanus and De Hoop *(see p101)* as well as False Bay *(see p33)* offer great vantage points to view the southern right whale breaching in deep, sheltered bays.

6 Duiker Island, Near Hout Bay

A flat granite outcrop, this island *(see p86)* supports a 5,000–6,000 strong colony of seals, three species of cormorant and some penguins. Boat tours run past the seal-lined shores.

Colony of seals at Duiker Island

7 Inverdoorn Game Reserve

A spectacular sight in the Karoo, Inverdoorn Game Reserve (see p71) is only a few hours' drive from Cape Town. It is rich in wildlife, including lion, cheetah, giraffe, antelope and white rhino. A range of leisure activities are also available.

8 Cape of Good Hope

The most southerly sector of Table Mountain National Park, the Cape of Good Hope (see pp32–3) boasts spectacular oceanic view-points. It also offers great wildlife watching – bontebok, grysbok and Cape mountain zebra coexist with the Chacma baboon, eland and small grey mongoose.

Baboons at the Cape of Good Hope

9 Dassies on Table Mountain

Cute, semi-tame dassies (rock hyraxes) sunbathe on Table Mountain (see pp22–3). Resembling guinea pigs, but larger and sharper-toothed, these oddball creatures are dwarfish relics of a group of ungulates that dominated the African herbivore niche about 35 million years ago.

10 Aquila Private Game Reserve

R46, Touws River (off the N1) ▪ 021 430 7260 ▪ www.aquilasafari.com
Inhabited by large animals including lion, elephant and buffalo, this reserve in the southern Karoo offers a wide variety of activities including day safaris from Cape Town, horse-back and quad-bike adventures, and overnight and fly-in options.

TOP 10 ENDEMIC FLORA AND FAUNA

The distinctive king protea bloom

1 King Protea
This pineapple-sized salmon-pink bloom is South Africa's national flower.

2 Red Disa
The "Pride of Table Mountain", this very pretty red flower blooms in December and January.

3 Silver Tree
Restricted to the Cape Peninsula, this protea-affiliated tree has silver-haired stems and cone-like flowers.

4 African Penguin
The only penguin that breeds in South Africa. Two other sub-Antarctic species sometimes turn up on Cape beaches.

5 Bontebok
This beautifully marked antelope was on the verge of extinction in the early 20th century, but the species has since recovered (see p102).

6 Cape Dwarf Chameleon
The most readily observed of four chameleon species living in the Western Cape mountains.

7 Cape Mountain Zebra
Rescued from extinction, the Cape Mountain Zebra has fared better than its close relative, the quagga, which was hunted out in the 19th century.

8 Cape Sugarbird
This long-tailed fynbos dweller belongs to a family whose range is limited to South Africa and Zimbabwe.

9 Orange-Breasted Sunbird
A dazzling nectar-eater that only lives in flowering fynbos habitats.

10 Table Mountain Ghost Frog
This club-fingered frog is restricted to several streams on the eastern and southern slopes of the mountain.

🔟 Viewpoints

View of the Lion's Head and Central Cape Town from Signal Hill

1 Signal Hill

Accessible by car or foot and rising between the City Bowl and Sea Point, the flat-topped 350-m (1,148-ft) Signal Hill (see p70) is an extension of a taller, hornlike rock formation known as Lion's Head. From Signal Hill Road, viewpoints overlook the eastern side of the city, while the picnic site at the top affords views over Table Bay and the Atlantic Seaboard. It is one of the best spots in Cape Town to watch a sunset in the red western sky.

2 Rhodes Memorial

Situated on the eastern slopes of Table Mountain, this is a rather bombastic memorial (see p80) to the former Cape Prime Minister. The views over the Cape Flats to distant Helderberg and the Hottentots Holland Mountains are best enjoyed from the adjacent restaurant.

3 Rooikrans

In the far south of the Table Mountain National Park, this underutilized viewpoint (see p32) provides a thrilling north-facing vantage over the False Bay seaboard. There are also great whale watching opportunities between June and November.

4 Chapman's Peak Drive

One of the world's most spectacular marine drives, this toll road (see p86) was constructed in 1915–22 along the band of shale that divides the granite base of Chapman's Peak from

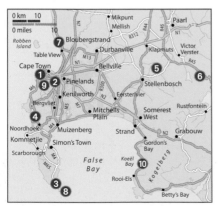

the overlying sandstone. It winds along the mountainside between Hout Bay and Noordhoek with viewpoints along the way. Stop to admire the sheer cliffs of Chapman's Peak and the Atlantic battering the shore below.

5 Tokara Wine Estate

At the crest of Helshoogte Pass, this wine and olive estate (see p36) boasts perhaps the most scenic location in the Winelands. The views stretch across eucalyptus-swathed slopes to False Bay and – on a clear day – distant Table Mountain. Best enjoyed with a chilled glass of one of the estate's crisp Sauvignon Blanc wines.

6 Franschhoek Pass
MAP F2

This pass is often ignored by tourists in the Winelands because it leads to remote Villiersdorp rather than trendy Stellenbosch. But it is worth following this road for a couple of kilometres to take in the lovely views over the thatched rooftops and the expansive vineyards that are located in the Franschhoek Valley (see pp36–7).

7 Bloubergstrand
MAP B2

About 10 km (6 miles) north of Cape Town, the Bloubergstrand beach hems in Table Bay on the West Coast. This "Blue Mountain Beach" is named after the flat-topped Table Mountain, which looms over its sandy expanse. Usually at its prettiest in the morning, the beach is also a lovely place to visit in the afternoon, when you can enjoy the vista from its alfresco cafés.

Kitesurfers on Bloubergstrand beach

8 Cape Point

Situated at the southern tip of the Cape Peninsula within the Cape of Good Hope (see pp32–3), Cape Point is reached via a steep footpath or a chuffing funicular. The views include Atlantic-battered cliffs and beaches and an open seascape that stretches all the way south to Antarctica.

The sea-worn cliffs at Cape Point

9 Table Mountain Upper Cableway

Within 15 minutes of the Upper Cableway station (see p22), a succession of viewpoints reveal the geography of the Western Cape, from nearby Signal Hill to surf-splashed Robben Island and False Bay, all overshadowed by the Hottentots Holland Mountains. No less impressive are the views across the Cape Peninsula's mountainous spine to Cape Point.

10 Clarence Drive
MAP D4–5

Hugging the cliffy coast between Gordon's Bay and Rooi-Els, Clarence Drive is one of the most spectacularly beautiful roads in South Africa, and, luckily, viewpoints abound. Look out, too, for baboons along the way.

TOP 10 Beaches

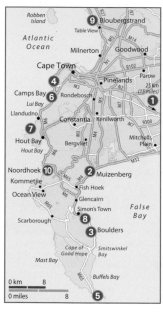

make it very popular with families. If the sunbathing gets too monotonous, there are also some great tidal rock pools at Gordon's Bay.

2 Muizenberg

Situated on the northern shore of False Bay, Muizenberg *(see p85)* has been a seaside resort and Cape Town's premier surfing beach since the 1920s. Facilities include a protected pool, waterslides, mini-golf, snack shops and colourful huts. The beach is safe for swimming and hence, is a favourite with families. It is also very accessible by train from the city centre.

Colourful Muizenberg beach huts

1 Bikini Beach, Gordon's Bay

MAP D4

Less than an hour's drive east of Cape Town, secluded Bikini Beach is the most popular of the many beaches around Strand. Overlooked by the Helderberg Mountains, it offers clear views across False Bay. The shallow waters are safe for swimming, and an abundance of restaurants and cafés

3 Boulders Beach

This is a lovely, secluded beach *(see p30)* on the southern fringe of the penguin colony. Enjoy the company of these remarkable birds, who bustle fearlessly around the same rocks where tourists sunbathe. An entrance fee is required.

Penguins at Boulders Beach

View over Clifton's Fourth Beach

4 Clifton Beach

Within very easy walking distance of Sea Point and Green Point, perennially fashionable Clifton *(see p70)* is the closest swimming beach to the city centre. Of the four sandy coves, divided by granite out-crops, Fourth Beach has the best facilities, including changing rooms, public toilets, snack and soda kiosks. Deck chairs and umbrellas are available for rental. The waters are chilly and the undertow should not be underestimated.

5 Cape of Good Hope

Set below Cape Point, this windswept beach *(see pp32–3)* is arguably the most beautiful on the peninsula. As well as attracting sunbathers and swimmers, the Cape is also a magnet for walkers and nature enthusiasts.

6 Camps Bay

Overlooked by the spectacular Twelve Apostles formation on the western face of Table Mountain, this wide, sandy beach *(see p68)* lies alongside the main road through Camps Bay, below a row of street cafés, restaurants and bars. Popular with families over the holidays, it is quieter at other times. Deckchairs and parasols are available for hire.

7 Sandy Bay
MAP G2

Protected by high dunes and dotted with secluded rocky coves for sun-bathing, Sandy Bay near Llandudno has long been a semi-official nudist beach. It also hosts something of a gay scene, although by no means exclusively so. It is not accessible by public transport, and is often too chilly for swimming.

8 Seaforth Beach

Like nearby Boulders, this beach, within walking distance of Simon's Town, is hemmed in by gigantic rocks. Generally, it is not too busy, and there's a chance of spotting stray penguins waddling past. The charming Seaforth Restaurant with its wooden balcony overlooks the beach *(see p31)*.

9 Bloubergstrand

The *blouberg* (blue mountain) is Table Mountain *(see pp22–3)*, whose flat-topped profile is displayed in full glory on a clear day. Sandy for the most part, Bloubergstrand *(see p49)* has enough rocky protrusions to keep it interesting. Rather exposed in windy weather, the beach is a favourite for watersports.

10 Noordhoek

Below Chapman's Peak *(see p86)*, Noordhoek *(see p87)* is a seemingly endless arc of glorious white sand near Kommetjie. Although too exposed to the elements to host much of a beach scene, it attracts walkers, bird-watchers and horse riders. It's also perfect for a long seaside stroll.

Sunset at Noordhoek Beach

TOP 10 Adventure Activities

A rock climber in the Western Cape

1 Rock Climbing
City Rock: 021 447 1326; call ahead to book; www.cityrock.co.za
The craggy Western Cape peaks are a rock-climber's paradise. City Rock is the leading centre to visit for a good selection of climbing gear or experienced instructors. It also has an indoor climbing centre.

2 Ocean Kayaking
Offering a fascinating view of the scenic Cape Peninsula, daily ocean kayaking excursions run out of Simon's Town and Hout Bay, weather permitting. While kayaking, you're likely to encounter marine animals such as penguins and seals.

3 Caving
Cape Peninsula Spelaeological Society (CPSS): www.caving.org.za
The sandstone caverns above Kalk Bay are reached via a steep footpath, which offers views over False Bay. The earliest evidence of human habitation at the Cape was excavated here. Some clambering and crawling is required to explore the cavernous depths. Do carry a torch.

4 Kitesurfing
Cabrinha: 021 554 1729; www.cabrinha.co.za
Cape Town is known for its windy weather, which, along with the might of the Atlantic Ocean, makes it perfect for kitesurfing. There's always a group of kitesurfers at Muizenberg beach, but the best locations are Blouberg and Big Bay in Table Bay.

5 Scuba Diving
Scuba Shack: 072 603 8630; www.scubashack.co.za
The coast to the north of Durban is renowned for its offshore reefs teeming with colourful fish. However, the chillier waters off Cape Town also provide great diving possibilities – immense forests of swaying kelp, friendly seals on the Atlantic Seaboard, and a large number of shipwrecks to be explored.

Kayaking at Boulders Beach, Simon's Town

6 Winelands Ballooning

021 863 3192; runs Nov–Apr only, weather permitting; www.kapinfo.com

A blissful way to start the day is to glide over the beautiful winelands around Paarl at sunrise in a hot-air balloon. Afterwards, a support vehicle takes you back to Paarl for a champagne breakfast.

7 Kloofing

Absolute Adventures: 074 620 1525; www.absoluteadventures.co.za

Kloofing – also known as canyoning – is a uniquely Western Cape extreme adventure. The guided excursion involves hiking, boulder-hopping, wading through fast-moving rivers and jumping into pools from cliffs up to 15 m (49 ft) high. The best sites such as the ominously named Suicide Gorge and Kamikaze Kanyon are in the mountains outside of the city.

8 Abseiling

Abseil Africa: 073 065 1520; www.abseilafrica.co.za

For spectacular heart-stopping views from Table Mountain, take in Abseil Africa's 112-m (367-ft) controlled descent of the western face. It is considered the world's highest commercial abseil.

9 Quad Biking

Downhill Adventures: 021 422 0388; www.downhilladventures.com

The natural beauty in and around Cape Town makes it a great place for quad biking. Experienced guides will show you how to operate the bike before taking you on a ride across the Cape Peninsula and the Winelands.

10 Paragliding

Para-Pax: 082 881 4724; www.parapax.co.za

Tandem paragliding from Signal Hill or Lion's Head offers stunning views of Cape Town's Atlantic Seaboard suburbs and Table Bay. No prior experience is required for the enjoyable glide as you are clipped into the pilot's harness. Visit the website for more details.

TOP 10 WALKS

The scenic Sea Point Promenade

1 Sea Point Promenade
Take a stroll along the Promenade, Sea Point's most famous landmark.

2 Nursery Ravine and Skeleton Gorge
This challenging hike begins in Kirstenbosch National Botanical Garden *(see pp26–7)* and follows a steep pathway to Maclear's Beacon *(see p23)*.

3 Green Point Urban Park
Wander around this beautiful park *(see p61)* and admire the unique sculptures that dot the Biodiversity Garden.

4 Pipe Track
This relatively easy trail, below the spectacular Twelve Apostles range, affords panoramic views of Camps Bay.

5 Kalk Bay
The mountains above Kalk Bay *(see p87)* offer numerous hiking trails with magnificent views of False Bay.

6 Newlands Forest
Situated on the eastern slopes of Table Mountain, this forest offers hiking tracks of varying levels of difficulty.

7 Company's Garden
Amble through the garden *(see pp12–13)* to spot the local grey squirrels.

8 Lion's Head
This iconic peak offers great views of the Atlantic and has one of the city's most popular hiking trails *(see p60)*.

9 Chapman's Peak
Hike above Chapman's Peak for amazing views of the Atlantic Ocean, Hout Bay and Fish Hoek *(see p85)*.

10 Cape Point
A hiker's paradise, Cape Point *(see p49)* has many trails with stunning scenery, including deserted beaches, battered cliffs and local wildlife.

⏫10 Sports and Outdoor Activities

① Rugby
Newlands Stadium: MAP J2; 021 659 4600; www.wprugby.com

Traditionally one of the world's best teams, the South African "Springboks" have won the Rugby World Cup thrice (in 1995, 2007 and 2019). International matches are held at Newlands Stadium, home to Western Province and the Stormers Super Rugby teams.

Springboks playing rugby

② Kayaking in False Bay
Kayak Cape Town: 065 707 4444; www.kayakcapetown.co.za

Starting from Simon's Town, ideally on a windless day, paddle through scenic False Bay, and look for penguins, dolphins and whales.

③ Golf
Rondebosch Golf Club: MAP H1; 021 689 4176; www.rondebosch golfclub.com ■ Steenberg Golf Club: MAP H3; 021 713 2233; www.steenberggolfclub.co.za

There are several golf courses in Cape Town. Two of the best are Rondebosch Golf Club and the Steenberg Golf Club.

④ Cricket
Newlands Cricket Stadium: MAP H2; 021 657 2000; www. newlandscricket.com

Newlands is one of the world's most beautiful cricket grounds with Table Mountain and Devil's Peak as a backdrop. It's home to the Western Cape's provincial team and regularly hosts One Day International, T20 and Test matches.

⑤ Deep-Sea Fishing
Hooked on Africa: 021 790 5332; www.hookedonafrica.co.za ■ Big Blue Fishing Charters: 082 362 6294; www. bigbluefishingcharters.com

The waters off the Cape Peninsula are renowned for their great deep-sea fishing, with tuna being a speciality. Charters depart from the harbours at Hout Bay or Simon's Town.

⑥ Horse Riding, Noordhoek
Horse Riding Cape Town: 076 251 8564; www.horseridingcapetown.com

The sandy Noordhoek Beach below Chapman's Peak is great for horse riding. Lessons are available for all ages, as well as specially abled riders.

⑦ Hiking
Ridgeway Ramblers: 082 522 6056; www.ridgwayramblers.co.za

Hiking trails suitable for all levels of fitness traverse most of the nature reserves and national parks. Most can be walked unguided, but there's also the option of going with an experienced guide.

Hikers looking down on Hout Bay

Mountain biking

8 Mountain Biking
Downhill Adventures: 021 422 0388; www.downhilladventures.com
The mountainous Winelands offer great opportunities for cyclists. Bikes can be hired in all the main centres, and several reserves have trails.

9 Surfing
Gary's Surf School: Muizenberg; 021 788 9839; www.garysurf.co.za
The Western Cape offers some of the world's best surfing, with schools providing lessons and board and wet-suit hire. Muizenberg, on False Bay, is a reliable place to learn. Sites along the Atlantic seaboard, while less busy, are more challenging.

10 Football
Cape Town Stadium: MAP N1; capetownstadium.co.za
Cape Town Spurs and Cape Town City FC represent the city in South Africa's Premier Soccer League. They play home matches at Cape Town Stadium.

TOP 10 SOUTH AFRICAN SPORTING ICONS

1 Ernie Els
The former world number-one golfer, better known as the Big Easy, has won four major titles.

2 Kagiso Rabada
In 2018, aged 23, Rabada became the youngest ever bowler to take 150 test wickets, topping the official test and ODI bowler rankings in the process.

3 Benni McCarthy
His 32 international goals while playing for the national team Bafana Bafana (1997–2012) are a South African record.

4 Francois Pienaar
He captained the South African rugby team, which won the 1995 Rugby World Cup on its home turf.

5 Liezel Huber
This tennis doubles specialist won five women's and two mixed doubles Grand Slam titles between 2005 and 2011.

6 Siya Kolisi
Kolisi led South Africa to victory in the 2019 Rugby World Cup final.

7 Penny Heyns
Winner of both the 100-m and 200-m breaststroke in the 1996 Olympics, Penny Heyns was the first ever woman to win gold in both races.

8 Lucas Radebe
Former South Africa and Leeds captain, he played in the football team that won the 1996 Africa Nations Cup.

9 Gary Player
One of the all-time golfing greats, Player has also designed golf courses in South Africa and around the world.

10 Caster Semenya
She won an Olympic gold medal at Rio 2016 for the women's 800-m race.

Caster Semenya in action

Children's Attractions

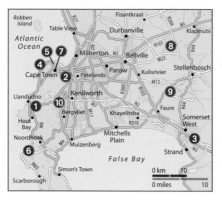

harp, logic puzzles and human gyroscope. There's a café serving light meals.

3 Table Mountain Cableway

Since climbing Table Mountain on foot could be too demanding for most youngsters, taking the cableway to the summit (see p22) is highly recommended. The cable car rotates a full 360 degrees, offering spectacular views over the city bowl and Table Bay. Once at the top, you can relax at a self-catering café and watch the resident hyraxes.

1 World of Birds

MAP G2 ■ Valley Rd, Hout Bay
■ 021 790 2730 ■ Open 9am–5pm daily
■ Adm ■ www.worldofbirds.org.za

Situated in Hout Bay, this is Africa's largest bird park with over 400 indigenous and exotic species, including parrots and barbets. Visitors can follow the stages of birdlife, right from eggs in incubation to the feeding of chicks.

4 Blue Train Park

MAP M1 ■ Beach Rd, Mouille Point ■ 084 314 9200
■ Open 9:30am–6:30pm Tue–Sun
■ Adm ■ www.thebluetrainpark.co.za

There are all sorts of things to keep little ones entertained at this impressive outdoor park, including bouncy castles, jungle gyms, a mini bike track, a climbing wall and even a simulated ice-skating rink. The miniature train that gives the park its name makes constant loops around the edge of the park, with one ride per person included in the entrance fee.

World of Birds

2 Cape Town Science Centre

MAP H1 ■ 370B Main Rd, Observatory
■ 021 300 3200 ■ Open 9am–4:30pm
Mon–Sat, 10am–4:30pm Sun ■ Adm
■ www.ctsc.org.za

This is the perfect place to head on a rainy day. There are more than 250 interactive exhibits to keep kids of all ages entertained. Little ones love the electric model train set and the chance to build a wall with foam bricks, while older kids (and adults) favour things such as the stringless

The miniature train in Blue Train Park

The beach section of the penguin exhibit at Two Oceans Aquarium

5 Two Oceans Aquarium

South Africa's leading aquarium, Two Oceans (see p14) has an extraordinary diversity of marine life from the Atlantic and the warmer Indian Ocean. The penguins, sharks and giant rays are favourites with children. A free activity centre hosts puppet shows and arts and crafts.

6 Imhoff Farm

MAP G4 ■ Kommetjie ■ 021 783 4545 ■ Open 9am–5pm Sun–Tue, 9am–10pm Wed–Sat ■ www.imhoff farm.co.za

This restored 18th-century farm en route to Cape Point has domestic animals roaming the Higgeldy Piggeldy Farmyard and a double-storey wooden maze.

7 Iziko Planetarium

The domed planetarium, part of the Iziko South African Museum complex (see p13) in the Company's Garden, features daily shows introducing the brilliant southern night sky. There are also shows for kids.

8 Wild Clover Farm

MAP D2 ■ R304, Stellenbosch ■ 021 865 2219 ■ Open 9am–5pm Tue–Sun ■ www.wildclover.co.za

With little bikes, pony rides, archery and game drives to see wildlife, Wild Clover is one of the best places for families in the Winelands. For the grown-ups there's a microbrewery and a small winery, plus a restaurant and self-catering accommodation.

9 Spier Wine Farm

The most child-friendly of the Cape wine estates, Spier Wine Farm (see p92) has a number of playgrounds and an exciting eagle-encounter programme with falconry displays as well as the chance for encounters with Wahlberg's and Verreaux's eagles.

Child-friendly Spier Wine Farm

10 The Bike Park at Constantia Uitsig

MAP H2 ■ 3347 Spaanschemat River Rd, Constantia ■ 081 833 4488 ■ Open 9am–5pm daily ■ www.bike parkatuitsig.co.za

Designed and built by Chris Nixon, a former South African mountain-bike champion, this fun bike park at Constantia Uitsig is suitable for all ages and levels of skill, from toddlers on balance bikes to professionals. Specific areas of the park have been dedicated to focusing on different biking skills.

🔟 Wining and Dining

Exclusive dining in La Petite Colombe

1 La Petite Colombe

Now based at the suburban Leeu Estates, this fine-dining restaurant is perfect for splurging on a special occasion. Diners sit down to a five- or nine-course feast that showcases local flavours and seasonal produce. Both course menus are available as vegetarian or non-vegetarian options.

2 Den Anker Restaurant and Bar

Set on a small jetty, Den Anker (see p76) is one of the Waterfront's top eateries, serving Belgian specialities, local seafood including West Coast crayfish and great European draft beers. Outdoor tables have a view of seals and boats in the harbour with Table Mountain as a backdrop.

3 La Colombe

This elegant, first-class restaurant (see p81) is rated as one of Cape Town's best. The multi-course menus feature top-quality local ingredients that are given a French touch, with a dash of Asian fusion. Book early for a table on the balcony with forest and mountain views.

4 The Test Kitchen

This is widely considered the best restaurant (see p77) on the continent. Plan months ahead if you want to sample the multi-course tasting menu. Tables at the sister restaurant, The Pot Luck Club, are easier to obtain.

5 Kleine Zalze Restaurant

Classic pairings can make dishes appear simple, but the chef at this establishment (see p98) knows how to bring out the flavours of the seasonal produce. Take your cue from the slow cooking methods and make it a long dining experience, enhanced by estate wines.

6 Gold Restaurant

At the unabashedly touristy Gold Restaurant (see p77), you'll taste traditional delicacies from across

African-inspired dishes at Gold

Africa during a 14-course banquet. Music and dance accompanies your meal, and you are even scattered with 24-carat gold dust before you leave.

7 Jordan Restaurant

Contemporary dishes at this restaurant (see p98) feature local meats and seafood, such as West Coast mussels and springbok, and chef George Jardine changes the seasonal menu daily. Vast windows maximize the views of the dam, surrounding vineyards and mountains.

8 Kloof Street House

One of Cape Town's trendiest eateries, Kloof Street (see p77) is set in a restored Victorian house. The historic setting is offset by a funky interior, and the imaginative menu is strong on game, shellfish and vegetarian dishes.

Eclectic interior of Kloof Street House

9 The Foodbarn

Many of Cape Town's best chefs cite Franck Dangereux – owner and chef of The Foodbarn – as their mentor, after his previous work at La Colombe. Expect superb French-influenced food, sublime sauces and boutique wines here (see p89) in Noordhoek Farm Village.

10 Picnics at Boschendal

Something about the Winelands invites lingering picnics with chilled white wine. No estate offers this with as much panache as Boschendal (see p36), where you can enjoy local artisanal goodies in a super-scenic picnic spot.

TOP 10 SOUTH AFRICAN DISHES AND DELICACIES

Cape Malay bobotie

1 Bobotie
A Cape Malay classic of minced beef and yellow rice, sweetened by raisins and topped with an egg sauce.

2 Potjiekos
This dish features meat and vegetables cooked slowly in a *potjie* (a cast-iron black pot) over an open fire.

3 Waterblommetjie Bredie
A Cape stew made of lamb and *waterblommetjie*, a water plant that resembles an artichoke.

4 Tomato Bredie
A thick, tasty tomato-based stew made of succulent Karoo lamb.

5 Boerewors
Spicy, fatty "farmer's sausage", best *braaied* (barbecued) on an open fire.

6 Malva Pudding
This sweet, spongy Dutch pudding contains apricot jam and is served hot.

7 Melktert
This dish is a milkier and sweeter version of a custard tart. Dates back to Cape Malay-Dutch cooking.

8 Biltong
Spicy strips of dried, salted and spiced raw beef or game, biltong is reminiscent of beef jerky.

9 Pap 'n' Stew
The traditional staple in most of South Africa, this is a meat stew that is eaten along with *mealie pap* (a porridge made from ground maize).

10 Koeksisters
Translated as "cake sisters", these are doughnut-like spiral pastries with a sticky-sweet coating.

Koeksisters

TOP10 Cape Town and the Winelands for Free

Views from Oranjezicht City Farm

① Oranjezicht City Farm
MAP P6 ▪ Upper Orange St, Oranjezicht, Cape Town ▪ 083 508 1066 ▪ Open 8am–4pm Mon–Fri, 9am–2pm Sat ▪ www.ozcf.co.za
Located on the site of a historic farm, this non-profit urban farm on the slopes of Table Mountain is a joy to explore. Guided tours are available for a small donation. The farm's organic market takes place each Saturday and Sunday at Granger Bay.

② V&A Waterfront
There is plenty of action to keep you engaged during a relaxed stroll around the V&A Waterfront (see p14–15). Seals cavort in the harbour, gulls soar overhead, and the complex is studded with historic landmarks, statues and benches where you can sit, relax and watch the world go by.

③ Company's Garden
There's plenty to see for free in this glorious city park (see pp12–13), including an aviary, the 18th-century façade of the president's official Cape Town residence, and a range of monuments and memorials.

④ Coastal Walk from Muizenberg to Kalk Bay
The 3-km (2-mile) walk from Muizenberg's Edwardian train station (see p85) to Kalk Bay (see p87) hugs the coast. Take a dip in the tidal pool at St James; browse Kalk Bay's galleries and shops; and end up at the harbour, where fishermen and seals vie for the same rewards.

⑤ City Walking Tours
City Sightseeing: 0861 733 287; www.citysightseeing.co.za
The company in charge of open-top bus trips also offers free 90-minute walking tours taking in historically significant neighbourhoods. Amble through Company's Garden, wander the colourful houses of the Bo-Kaap or take a city centre stroll visiting Greenmarket Square and City Hall.

⑥ Climbing Lion's Head
MAP K6
You don't need money to get to the top of Lion's Head, but you do need a head for heights. The peak is 669-m- (2,195-ft-) high, and the 2-hour round-trip hike is strenuous, involving chains and ladders. Join the locals for a full-moon night hike.

Lion's Head peak

7 The Noon Gun

Clamber up Signal Hill from Bo-Kaap and take your place behind the safety line to witness this cannon herald the arrival of noon. It has been fired each day except Sunday since 1806, and there has only been one recorded instance of both main and backup gun failing.

8 Green Point Urban Park

A stone's throw from the ocean, this park *(see p70)* is a magnificent place to wander, cycle or picnic in. You can admire indigenous plants and modern sculptures, get lost in the labyrinth and indulge in a little bird-watching. There's a superb playground for children and an outdoor gym for the grown-ups.

Green Point Urban Park

9 Woodstock Street Art
MAP H1

This once run-down industrial district is now a creative hub filled with galleries, quirky boutiques, craft breweries and micro-distilleries. Woodstock is also home to an eclectic collection of murals featuring political, cultural and environmental messages.

10 Parliament Tours
MAP Q5 ■ 100 Plein St, Cape Town ■ 021 403 2266 ■ Open 9am–noon Mon–Fri (tours hourly) ■ www.parliament.gov.za

Learn all about the history of South Africa's parliament on an hour-long tour. Be sure to book in advance and bring your passport along on the day.

TOP 10 BUDGET TIPS

Free waterfront entertainment

1 Look out for free concerts at the V&A Waterfront year-round and in De Waal Park throughout summer.

2 Visit in winter (May to August) for discounts on accommodation, transport and attractions.

3 GoCards *(www.gocards.co.za)* offer passes giving discounted or free entry to a number of attractions.

4 EatOut *(www.eatout.co.za)* keeps an up-to-date list of daily restaurant specials around the city.

5 Most of Cape Town's museums offer free entry on certain commemorative days. Iziko *(www.iziko.org.za)* has a complete list.

6 The MyCiti bus to Hout Bay is an equally scenic, cheaper alternative to the open-top City Sightseeing bus.

7 Keep hold of receipts – non-South Africans can claim VAT back.

8 Grab a free copy of *Coast to Coast* *(www.coasttocoast.co.za)*, a budget travel guide offering discounts.

9 Book online for attractions where possible – there's often a discount.

10 Many wineries offer tastings for a nominal fee, with no pressure to buy.

South African wine tasting

Festivals and Events

1 Kaapse Klopse
2 Jan

Also known as the Cape Minstrel Festival, this colourful *Tweede Nuwe Jaar* (Second New Year) celebration involves brightly attired minstrels organized into several *klopse* (clubs) that sing traditional tunes accompanied by a *ghoema* drum. It's great fun, but competition between *klopse* is intense.

2 Maynardville Open-Air Festival
MAP H2 ■ Maynardville Park, Wynberg ■ Jan–Mar ■ www.mayn ardville.co.za

Known for its annual Shakespeare-in-the-Park plays, this festival also includes symphony orchestra, ballet performances and stand-up comedy shows.

Festivalgoers at Kaapse Klopse

3 Stellenbosch Wine Festival
MAP D2 ■ Coetzenburg Sports Grounds ■ Feb ■ www.stellenbosch winefestival.co.za

This three-day event showcases more than 500 wines by Cape estates. The festival features special tasting rooms, gourmet food and live music.

4 Cape Town Pride Festival
Feb–Mar ■ www.capetownpride.org

Cape Town's most important LGBTQ+ festival was inaugurated in 2001. Pride Parade Day attracts a stream of colourful floats and involves drag shows, fashion events and an after party. The two-week festival also includes pageants, tea parties and gay movies.

5 Cape Town Carnival
MAP P2 ■ Somerset Rd, Green Point ■ 021 406 3584 ■ Mid-Mar ■ www.capetowncarnival.com

Held along Green Point's famous Fan Walk, this Rio-style carnival celebrates South Africa's diversity and culture. It features parades, magnificent floats, musicians, dance troupes and street parties.

6 Cape Town International Jazz Festival
021 671 0506 ■ Last weekend in Mar ■ www.capetownjazzfest.com

Hosted at the Cape Town International Convention Centre (CTICC) on five indoor and outdoor stages, the continent's largest jazz festival attracts more than 40 top local and international performers.

Musicians rocking the Cape Town International Jazz Festival

7 Oude Libertas Summer Season Festival

MAP D2 ■ Stellenbosch ■ 021 809 7380 ■ Oct–Mar ■ www.oudelibertas.co.za

This music festival is held at the Oude Libertas Estate on the Papegaaiberg. It has an eclectic programme featuring traditional chamber music, jazz and *boeremusiek* (Afrikaans folk).

8 Cape Town Festival of Beer

MAP N1 ■ Hamilton's Rugby Club, Green Point ■ Late Nov ■ www.capetownfestivalofbeer.co.za

A three-day event at which microbrewers from across the country join with major brands to offer their wares to a thirsty public.

Kirstenbosch Summer Sunset Concerts

9 Kirstenbosch Summer Sunset Concerts

MAP H2 ■ Rhodes Drive, Newlands ■ 021 799 8783 ■ Nov–Apr ■ www.sanbi.org/event_cat/kirstenbosch

A wonderful way to enjoy a Sunday sunset. The open-air concerts appeal to all musical tastes and take place within the beautiful botanic gardens.

10 Franschhoek Cap Classique and Champagne Festival

MAP F2 ■ Early Dec ■ www.franschhoekmcc.co.za

Celebrate the superb local wines made with the Champagne method at this event held at the Huguenot Monument. Top restaurants create dishes to pair with the bubbles.

TOP 10 SPORTING EVENTS

Racers at ABSA Cape Epic

1 L'Ormarins Queen's Plate
These horse races at Kenilworth Racecourse in January include hospitality events and fashion contests.

2 Cape Metropolitan Stakes
Held at the end of January at Kenilworth Racecourse, this high-profile event is a mix of fashion and horse-racing.

3 Quench Cape Town 10s
This multi-sport event held in February includes hockey, football and running. There's also live music and beer tents.

4 Discovery World Cup Triathlon Cape Town
Attracting professional and novice athletes over two days in February, this is part of the World Triathlon Series.

5 ABSA Cape Epic
A two-person team event featuring seven days of off-road mountain-bike racing through the Winelands in March.

6 Cape Town Cycle Tour
South Africa's largest individually timed cycling race, this attracts 35,000 on a 109-km (68-mile) route in March.

7 Old Mutual Two Oceans Marathon
This 56-km (35-mile) ultra-marathon, reputedly the most beautiful in the world, takes place over Easter Weekend.

8 Three Peaks Challenge
A trail running challenge ascending Devil's Peak, Table Mountain and Lion's Head. Held in November.

9 The Colour Run
This 5-km (3-mile) run in November is all about getting doused in coloured powder and the parties at the end.

10 The Twilight Team Run
A run/walk/skate in fancy-dress for 4 km (2 miles) in early December in the city centre. Raises money for charity.

Cape Town and the Winelands Area by Area

Spectacular view of Table Bay and Table Mountain from Bloubergstrand

TOP10 Central Cape Town

The historic heart of South Africa's oldest city is bound by Table Bay to the north and Table Mountain to the south. Signal Hill forms an imposing barrier between the City Bowl's inner city suburbs and those along the Atlantic. Cape Town's historic buildings, museums, theatres, restaurants and clubs, together with a buzzing street life, confirm the city's status as one of Africa's major cultural centres.

View over Cape Town

CENTRAL CAPE TOWN

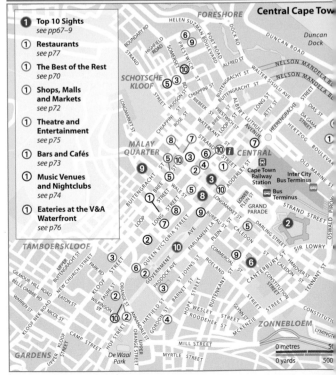

1. **Top 10 Sights**
   see pp67–9
1. **Restaurants**
   see p77
1. **The Best of the Rest**
   see p70
1. **Shops, Malls and Markets**
   see p72
1. **Theatre and Entertainment**
   see p75
1. **Bars and Cafés**
   see p73
1. **Music Venues and Nightclubs**
   see p74
1. **Eateries at the V&A Waterfront**
   see p76

1 Table Mountain

The 1,067-m (3,500-ft) high plateau of Table Mountain *(see pp22–3)* is reached by a rotating cablecar that offers 360° views across the city centre to the distant Hottentots Holland Mountains. At the top, a network of footpaths allows hikers to explore the *fynbos* vegetation. Maclear's Beacon, the highest summit, is less than an hour from the Upper Cableway Station. The more adventurous traveller might like to try Abseil Africa's controlled 112-m (367-ft) descent from a ledge overlooking Camps Bay.

2 Castle of Good Hope

Constructed in Table Bay between 1666 and 1679, Cape Town's oldest building – and a superbly

Guards at the Castle of Good Hope

preserved example of a Dutch East India Company fort – now stands inland as a result of land recla-mation. An imposing slate and sandstone pentagon *(see pp20–21)*, it has a rather utilitarian design that is alleviated by the sculpted masonry on the bell tower and the Anton Anreith bas-relief above the Kat Balcony. An interesting military museum and Dr William Fehr's Cape-based art collection are also housed here.

3 Greenmarket Square
MAP P4

This cobbled square in the heart of old Cape Town served as a slave market under the Dutch East India Company *(see p40)*, but its name alludes to its subsequent use as a fruit and vegetable market, which made way for a parking lot in the 1950s. Surrounded by historic build-ings, many housing smart cafés and eateries, it is now home to a popular pan-African craft market and lively street performers.

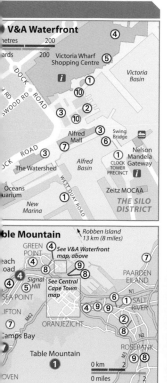

Locals relax in Greenmarket Square

4 Beach Road
MAP K3

Passing west of the city centre through the suburbs of Green Point and Sea Point, Beach Road runs along an attractive stretch of Atlantic coastline. The road is separated from the sea by a grassy promenade, where locals relax, jog and walk their dogs. It's great for a wander, especially at sunset. Don't miss the Green Point Lighthouse, the oldest in the country.

THE KHOE-SAN

When van Riebeeck established Cape Town in 1652 (see p40), the Western Cape had been inhabited by the Khoe-San-speaking populace for several millennia. Within 200 years they were gone; some had fallen victim to diseases, while others were killed by gun-toting settlers. Those who remained integrated into the mixed-race community, Cape Coloureds.

Green Point Lighthouse, Beach Road

5 V&A Waterfront

Cape Town's reconstituted harbour is also the city's foremost shopping venue (see pp14–15). Hundreds of shops, ranging from chain stores to quirky craft stalls, can be found alongside many restaurants and a host of tourist spots, including the Nelson Mandela Gateway. Boat and helicopter tour operators offer harbour cruises and flights over Table Mountain.

6 District Six Museum

This moving tribute to District Six, bulldozed in the apartheid era (see p40), is housed in the former Buitenkant Methodist Church, whose association with the anti-apartheid movement led to its forced closure in 1988. The museum's centrepiece is a vast, annotated floor map of the suburb in its multiracial heyday. Other exhibits in the museum (see pp18–19) tell of the cruelty and destructiveness of the racism that dominated South African life for almost half a century.

7 Camps Bay
MAP G1

Wonderfully set between mountain and sea, Camps Bay is where suburban Cape Town's Atlantic Seaboard gives way to the unspoilt coastal scenery of the Cape Peninsula. This idyllic suburb boasts one of the nicest beaches in greater Cape Town and has a fine range of restaurants and bars located on its waterfront.

The magnificent Camps Bay, set on the Atlantic coast

8 Old Town House
MAP P4 ▪ Greenmarket Square ▪ 021 481 3933 ▪ Open 9am–4pm daily ▪ Adm ▪ www.iziko.org.za

Built in 1755, the beautifully restored Old Town House served as the City Hall until 1905. Counted among the city's foremost architectural gems, it is a fabulous example of the early Cape Rococo architectural style, with a graceful triple-arched portico and a pretty belfry. It houses the renowned Michaelis Collection of paintings by Dutch and Flemish masters of the Golden Age (16th–18th centuries), which were donated to the city by Sir Max Michaelis in 1914.

Bo-Kaap's colourful houses

9 Bo-Kaap
MAP P4

The spiritual home of the Cape Malay community, Bo-Kaap (Upper Cape) is a vibrant neighbourhood in the city centre. Best known for its endlessly photogenic colourful houses, the area also has a small but interesting museum *(see p43)*. The best thing to do here, though, is to eat traditional Cape Malay cuisine. Seek out the local version of *koeksisters (see p59)*, or join a Cape Malay cooking class.

10 Company's Garden
Established in 1652 as a vegetable garden to provide fresh produce to Dutch East India Company ships docking at Table Bay, the Company's Garden *(see pp12–13)* doubles as a botanical garden. At the heart of Museum Mile, this inner-city park, with a backdrop of Table Mountain, is a great place for a stroll.

A DAY IN THE CITY CENTRE

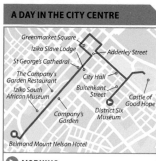

Greenmarket Square
Iziko Slave Lodge
St George's Cathedral
Adderley Street
The Company's Garden Restaurant
City Hall
Iziko South African Museum
Buitenkant Street
Castle of Good Hope
Company's Garden
District Six Museum
Belmond Mount Nelson Hotel

 MORNING

After breakfast, make your way to the **District Six Museum** *(see pp18–19)* and explore its stirring exhibits. Then walk a couple of blocks down **Buitenkant Street** to the **Castle of Good Hope** *(see pp20–21)* and join one of the free guided tours that run daily at 11am. At noon, return to the main gate for the firing of the signal cannon. Either drop in at the castle's two museums or enjoy a deli-style lunch at Re5 Restaurant. Afterwards, admire the **City Hall** *(see p21)* on the edge of the Grand Parade, where Mandela made his first public address after his release from prison in 1990. Then, walk across to **Adderley Street**, the city's principal shopping area, and take a detour to the curio market in **Greenmarket Square** on the way to **Company's Garden** *(see pp12–13)*.

AFTERNOON

If you didn't have lunch at the castle, and the weather's nice enough to eat alfresco, **The Company's Garden Restaurant** *(see p12)*, opposite the aviary, has to be first choice. Then take a stroll around the gardens, followed by a visit to one of the museums lining them, such as the **Iziko South African Museum** and the **Iziko Slave Lodge** *(see p13)*. If it's a gloomy day, visit **St George's Cathedral** *(see p13)* or take the kids to a show at the Planetarium *(see p13)* at the Iziko South African Museum. If you're feeling peckish, stroll to **Belmond Mount Nelson Hotel** *(see p114)* to sample its legendary tea buffet (2:30–5:30pm) before heading back to your hotel.

See map on pp66–7

The Best of the Rest

 St George's Mall
MAP Q4

Running through the heart of the historic city centre, this pedestrian mall is usually buzzing with street musicians and busy market stalls.

② Iziko South African Museum

Mainly featuring natural history displays, the South African Museum (see p13) also exhibits prehistoric rock art (see p42).

③ South African Jewish Museum
MAP P6 ■ 88 Hatfield St ■ 021 465 1546 ■ Open 10am–4pm Sun–Thu, 10am–2pm Fri ■ Adm ■ www. sajewishmuseum.co.za

This fascinating museum documents the history of South Africa's Jewish community. The complex also features the country's oldest synagogue, which dates back to 1863.

④ Green Point Urban Park
MAP M1 ■ Fritz Sonnenberg Rd ■ Open 7am–7pm daily

Part of a much larger development that includes the 2010 World Cup stadium, the park is a great leisure space. Nearby is the red-and-white-striped Green Point Lighthouse.

 Signal Hill
MAP M3

The climb or drive up Signal Hill is highly rewarding. Be there at sunset for stunning views over the Atlantic.

Signal Hill

⑥ Iziko Planetarium

The centrally located Planetarium (see p13) has daily shows introducing the dazzling southern sky – worthwhile for those heading into the Karoo, with its clear and brilliant night sky.

⑦ Lion's Head

A far more challenging goal than Signal Hill, Lion's Head (see p60) can only be reached on foot via a two-hour round hike that involves a vertiginous scramble using ladders to reach the summit. The views are worth the effort, especially at sunset.

⑧ Clifton Beaches
MAP A2

The closest beaches to the city centre, the four picturesque, sheltered coves at Clifton are divided by giant boulders.

White sands at a beach in Clifton

⑨ Church Square
MAP Q5

Flanked by grand old buildings on the west side stands the Groote Kerk, South Africa's oldest church. A monument marks the fact that enslaved people were once traded here.

⑩ Iziko Maritime Centre
MAP P1 ■ Union-Castle House, Dock Rd, V&A Waterfront ■ 021 405 2880 ■ Open 9am–4pm daily ■ Adm ■ www.iziko.org.za

Tracing the history of shipping in Table Bay, exhibits at this museum include model boats and photographs from the mail-ship era.

Organized Activities and Day Tours

African penguins at Boulders Beach

1 Cape Peninsula Day Tour
Organized tours to magnificent Cape Point also take in the Boulders Penguin Colony and include stops on the Atlantic Seaboard *(see pp32–3)*.

2 Cape Kayak Adventures
MAP M1 ■ 179 Beach Rd, Mouille Point ■ 083 346 1146 ■ www.kayak.co.za
Starting from Three Anchor Bay, this guided kayaking trip runs alongside the Sea Point Promenade *(see p53)*. The tour offers fantastic views of Lion's Head and Signal Hill as well as plenty of opportunities to spot dolphins, whales and seabirds.

3 City Sightseeing Bus
Cape Town open-top bus tours *(see pp112–13)* take in the city's main sights, while a separate route heads to Hout Bay and Constantia.

4 Wine-Tasting Tour
The ideal way to enjoy wine tasting is through the organized tours available out of Stellenbosch, Cape Town and Franschhoek.

5 District Six and Townships Tour
Typical tours of the townships *(see pp112–13)* start with a visit to the District Six Museum or Bo-Kaap, before moving on to the Langa and Khayelitsha townships. Lunch is at a local eatery or *shebeen* (bar).

6 Robben Island
Cape Town's most popular organized excursion is a guided tour of Robben Island *(see pp16–17)* via return boat trip from Nelson Mandela Gateway at the V&A Waterfront.

7 Whale- and Dolphin-Watching Cruise
Best undertaken in calm weather, cetacean-viewing excursions into Table Bay – though not as certain to produce whales as Hermanus – can be organized through kiosks lining the V&A Waterfront *(see pp14–15)*.

8 Duiker Island
A popular spot for boat excursions out of Hout Bay, Duiker Island *(see p46)* supports thousands of Cape fur seals and impressive numbers of marine birds.

9 Inverdoorn Game Reserve
MAP V3 ■ Off R46 ■ 021 422 0013 ■ www.inverdoorn.com
Set in the stunning Karoo, this reserve *(see p47)* boasts abundant wildlife, including white rhinos.

Giraffes at Inverdoorn Game Reserve

10 Table Mountain Day Hike
Hike Table Mountain ■ 060 539 9340 ■ www.hiketablemountain.co.za
Experienced hikers will enjoy the hiking possibilities offered at Table Mountain. All hikes are best undertaken with a knowledgeable local guide to avoid being caught out by sudden weather changes.

See map on pp66–7

Shops, Malls and Markets

1 V&A Waterfront
The Waterfront (see pp14–15) combines a wonderful harbourfront setting with a selection of shops and restaurants that is second to none.

2 Pan African Market
MAP Q4 ▪ 76 Long St ▪ 082 747 2308 ▪ Open 8:30am–5:30pm Mon–Fri (to 1:30pm Sat) ▪ www.panafrican.co.za

Mask, Pan African Market

Set in an old Victorian building, this indoor market is an excellent place to buy arts and crafts from all over Africa.

3 Cape Quarter
MAP P3 ▪ 27 Somerset Rd ▪ 021 421 1111 ▪ www.cape quarter.co.za

Cape Quarter has a historic location in the trendy De Waterkant suburb and houses shops specializing in crafts and jewellery. It also has several restaurants and cafés.

4 Long Street
MAP P5

Those seeking a colourful shopping experience will enjoy Long Street's cult, craft and second-hand shops.

5 Bree Street
MAP P4

Running through the heart of City Bowl, the trendy Bree Street features home decor and lifestyle shops as well as art galleries and cafés.

6 The Neighbourgoods Market
MAP H1 ▪ 373 Albert Rd, Woodstock ▪ Open 9am–3pm Sat ▪ www.neighbourgoodsmarket.co.za

This food market at the revived Old Biscuit Mill is the place to mingle with hip Capetonians on Saturdays.

7 Milnerton Flea Market
Marine Dr (R27) ▪ Open 8am–2pm Sat (to 3pm Sun) ▪ www.milnertonfleamarket.co.za

This eclectic market is a great place to find unusual items.

8 OZCF Market
MAP P1 ▪ Beach Rd, Granger Bay ▪ Open 9am–2pm Sat (to 3pm Sun)

As well as fresh produce from the Oranjezicht City Farm (see p60), you can buy freshly baked bread, artisanal cheese and free-range meat.

9 The Woodstock Exchange
MAP H1 ▪ 66–68 Albert Rd, Woodstock ▪ 021 486 5999 ▪ Open 8am–5pm Mon–Fri (to 2pm Sat) ▪ www.woodstockexchange.co.za

This uber-hip centre is home to young designers, artisans and other creatives. Pick up one-of-a-kind clothing or acquire a unique artwork.

Items at The Woodstock Exchange

10 Greenmarket Square
Situated on Greenmarket Square, Cape Town's oldest flea market (see p67) has a definite buzz about it. A variety of African crafts can be found alongside ethnically inspired clothing and jewellery.

Bars and Cafés

Sleek interior of the Bascule Whisky and Wine Bar

1 Bascule Whisky and Wine Bar

MAP Q2 ■ Cape Grace, West Quay Rd, V&A Waterfront ■ 021 410 7082

Enjoy South Africa's largest selection of whiskies at this waterfront bar. There's also a good wine list, beer on tap and whisky-tasting evenings.

2 Devil's Peak Taproom

MAP H1 ■ 150 Cecil Rd, Salt River ■ 021 203 0123

This chic, modern pub serves excellent beers by Devil's Peak Brewing Company. There's also an on-site brewery where guests can watch the brewers at work.

3 Mitchell's Scottish Ale House

MAP Q1 ■ East Pier & Dock Rd, V&A Waterfront ■ 021 419 5074

Mitchell's brews one of South Africa's most popular craft beers. The bar also hosts daily whisky tasting sessions.

4 Grand Café & Beach

MAP P1 ■ Haul Rd, Granger Bay ■ 021 425 0551

Enjoy a café-style dining experience on the deck or on the private beach with magnificent views of the ocean.

5 The Gin Bar

MAP P4 ■ 64a Wale St ■ 071 241 2277

This side-street bar serves only gin. Sit in the tiny courtyard and sip one of their four signature cocktails.

6 Sky Bar and Daddy Cool

MAP P4 ■ 38 Long St ■ 021 424 7247

The Sky Bar is on the rooftop terrace of the Grand Daddy Hotel, which offers Silver Bullet Airstream trailers for accommodation with a difference. Downstairs is the Daddy Cool Bar, where the decor is kitsch but trendy.

7 Beerhouse on Long Street

MAP P5 ■ 223 Long St ■ 079 369 8990

Enjoy Cape Town's biggest selection of local, international and craft beers in a pleasant, relaxing environment.

8 Souk

MAP P4 ■ 163 Long St ■ 060 682 6894

A contemporary gastro-pub, Souk serves delicious tapas and creative cocktails. There's a lovely balcony that overlooks Long Street.

9 Truth Coffee

MAP Q5 ■ 36 Buitenkant St ■ 021 200 0440

Cape Town's coolest coffee shop is as much about its steampunk style as it is about the perfect cup of coffee.

10 Planet Bar

MAP P6 ■ 76 Orange St ■ 021 483 1000

A sophisticated crowd frequents this bar at the Belmond Mount Nelson Hotel for after-work drinks. Outdoor tables overlook manicured grounds.

See map on pp66–7

Music Venues and Nightclubs

Traditional musicians playing at Mama Africa

① Mama Africa
MAP P5 ■ 178 Long St
■ 021 424 8634 ■ www.mamaafrica
restaurant.co.za

Traditional music accompanies a pan-African menu and lively African decor at this legendary bar and restaurant.

② The Waiting Room
MAP P5 ■ 273 Long St
■ 021 422 4536

Nestled above the Royale Eatery, this hip rooftop bar in the heart of Long Street hosts regular DJ nights and live music events.

③ Coco
MAP P4 ■ 70 Loop St ■ 072 673 6869 ■ www.cococpt.co.za

Book ahead for this upmarket club. Music varies depending on the day – expect house, hip hop, R & B and trance.

④ DecoDance
MAP L3 ■ 120 Main Rd, Sea Point ■ www.decodance.co.za

Cape Town's busiest nightclub plays retro rock and pop from the 1960s to the 1990s. No entry for under-22s.

⑤ The Piano Bar
MAP P3 ■ 47 Napier St, De Waterkant ■ 079 028 4628
■ www.thepianobar.co.za

Offering creative cocktails and tapas, this music revue bar has live entertainment and a wraparound terrace.

⑥ Dizzy's
MAP G1 ■ 41 The Drive, Camps Bay ■ 021 438 2686
■ www.dizzys.co.za

There's always something going on here, including karaoke, beer-pong tournaments and live bands.

⑦ The House of Machines
MAP P4 ■ 84 Shortmarket St
■ 021 422 0946

This small bar is known for its cocktails and craft beer. There is regular live music including open mic on Tuesday nights.

⑧ Alma Café
MAP H1 ■ 20 Alma Rd, Rosebank ■ 021 685 7377

Although it's a little outside the city centre, the Alma Café is worth a visit on Wednesday nights, when it hosts a burger 'n' beer evening with live music.

⑨ The Crypt Jazz Restaurant
MAP P4 ■ 1 Wale St ■ 063 680 6806 ■ www.cryptjazz.com

Based in the Crypt of St George's Cathedral, this restaurant has live jazz and a varied dinner menu.

⑩ Crew Bar
MAP P3 ■ 30 Napier St, Green Point ■ 073 204 3706

A vibrant gay bar offering top local music acts and stylish decor. It has a dance floor, VIP bar and verandahs.

See map on pp66–7

Theatre and Entertainment

(1) Artscape Theatre Centre
MAP R4 ▪ D F Malan St ▪ 021
410 9800 ▪ www.artscape.co.za
Cape Town's premier performing
arts complex hosts ballet, opera
and cabaret performances.

(2) Labia Cinema
MAP P6 ▪ 68 Orange St ▪ 021
424 5927 ▪ www.thelabia.co.za
This art cinema, named after its
benefactor, Princess Labia, shows
quality commercial movies and
special-interest films.

(3) Cape Town Comedy Club
MAP P2 ▪ 3 The Pumphouse,
V&A Waterfront ▪ 021 418 8880
▪ www.capetowncomedy.com
Steaks, pizzas and burgers are on
the menu, served with a side order
of home-grown comedy. You often
have to share a table, and you'll need
to book in advance for special offers.

(4) Stardust
MAP R5 ▪ 118 Sir Lowry Rd,
Woodstock ▪ 021 462 7777
▪ www.stardustcapetown.com
Between courses of Mediterranean
cuisine at this fun dinner-cabaret,
the serving staff take to the stage
to sing well-known covers.

(5) City Hall
MAP Q5 ▪ Darling St
▪ 021 410 9809 ▪ www.cpo.org.za
The impressive golden Italian
Renaissance-style City Hall is
the main concert venue for the
Cape Philharmonic Orchestra.

(6) Zip Zap Circus
MAP R4 ▪ 10 Jan Smuts St
▪ 021 421 8622 ▪ www.zip-zap.co.za
The city's non-profit circus school
puts on shows, with proceeds given
to social-outreach programmes.

(7) Theatre on the Bay
MAP G1 ▪ 1A Link Rd,
Camps Bay ▪ 021 438 3301
▪ www.pietertoerien.co.za
Stand-up comedy, musicals and
conventional farces are the staples
of this charming theatre.

(8) Magnet Theatre
MAP H1 ▪ Lower Main Rd,
Observatory ▪ 021 448 3436
▪ www.magnettheatre.co.za
As well as theatre and dance,
this venue offers social-upliftment
programs, and many performers
are young students from the area.

(9) Baxter Theatre
MAP H1 ▪ Main Rd, Rondebosch
▪ 021 685 7880 ▪ www.baxter.co.za
The Baxter has long been at the
cutting edge of local theatre. It shows
both mainstream productions and
more challenging works.

**(10) Pink Flamingo
Rooftop Cinema**
MAP P5 ▪ 38 Long St ▪ 021 207
8888 ▪ www.granddaddy.co.za
Cape Town's only outdoor cinema
is this delightfully retro rooftop
50-seater at the Granddaddy
Boutique Hotel. Booking in
advance is essential.

Magnificent City Hall

Eateries at the V&A Waterfront

Sevruga's bright verandah

1 Sevruga
MAP Q1 ▪ Shop 4, Quay 5
▪ 021 421 5134 ▪ RRR

A large and varied menu of good-quality dishes and an extensive wine list of mainly local producers.

2 Quay Four
MAP Q1 ▪ 4 Dock Rd
▪ 021 419 2008 ▪ RR

Two dining choices are on offer here. The Tavern offers pub fare, wooden tables and benches at the water's edge, while Upstairs at Quay Four is a more elegant option.

3 La Parada
MAP Q2 ▪ Alfred Mall
▪ 021 418 3003 ▪ RR

The lunch menu features upmarket bistro fare as well as a good selection of tapas. Popular for weekend brunch with good Table Mountain views.

4 Willoughby & Co
MAP Q1 ▪ 6130 & 6132 Victoria Wharf Centre ▪ 021 418 6115 ▪ RRR

Seafood is the speciality at this place, which is particularly noted for its sushi and the selection of wines by the glass.

5 Baia Seafood Restaurant
MAP Q1 ▪ 6262 Victoria Wharf Centre ▪ 021 421 0935 ▪ RRR

This bright restaurant serves top-notch seafood and meat dishes. These are best enjoyed from the balcony with its fine views of Table Mountain.

6 Den Anker Restaurant and Bar
MAP Q2 ▪ Pierhead ▪ 021 419 0249 ▪ RR

This restaurant has a great seafront location and serves beer, mussels and other Belgian specialities.

7 Ginja
MAP P2 ▪ Dock Rd ▪ 021 419 6677 ▪ RRR

The terrace seats at this restaurant offer gorgeous views over the harbour. Seafood, gourmet burgers and a long cocktail list are highlights of the menu.

8 Panama Jacks
MAP H1 ▪ Cruise Ship Terminal, Cape Town Harbour ▪ 021 448 1080 ▪ RR

This popular seafood restaurant lets diners select lobsters from seawater tanks. It also has great views of the incoming ships and the waterfront.

9 Makers Landing
MAP H1 ▪ Cruise Ship Terminal, Cape Town Harbour ▪ www.makers landing.co.za ▪ R

A farm-to-fork incubator with a market and restaurants serving authentic local food. It also has a microbrewery and distillery.

10 Harbour House
MAP P1 ▪ Quay 4, 280 Dock Rd
▪ 021 418 4744 ▪ RRR

Superlative seafood dominates the menu at this Cape Town favourite (with a branch in Kalk Bay). Be sure to try the catch of the day.

Alfresco dining at Harbour House

Restaurants

PRICE CATEGORIES
For a three-course meal for one, including half a bottle of wine, cover charge, taxes and extra charges.

R under R300 **RR** R300–400 **RRR** over R400

1 The Test Kitchen
MAP H1 ■ 375 Albert Rd, Woodstock ■ 021 447 2337 ■ RRR

An award-winning and world-renowned restaurant. Test Kitchen's dedicated executive chef Luke Dale-Roberts serves inventive global-style cuisine. Book months ahead.

2 Lord Nelson Restaurant
MAP P6 ■ 76 Orange St ■ 021 483 1000 ■ RRR

Belmond Mount Nelson Hotel is one of Cape Town's "grande dames", with an elegant atmosphere that attracts a well-heeled clientele. The restaurant offers a South African twist on international cuisine.

3 Kloof Street House
MAP N5 ■ 30 Kloof St, Gardens ■ 021 423 4413 ■ RRR

Set in a 20th-century Victorian house, this charming restaurant (see p59) has a brasserie-style menu that features contemporary dishes with a South African twist.

4 Aubergine Restaurant
MAP P6 ■ 39 Barnet St, Gardens ■ 021 465 0000 ■ RRR

This restaurant serves seafood, meat and vegetarian dishes with African, European and Asian influences.

5 Bukhara
MAP P4 ■ 33 Church St ■ 021 424 0000 ■ RRR

Cape Town's top Indian restaurant, Bukhara has a fabulous vegetarian selection on its menu.

6 Beluga
MAP P3 ■ The Foundry, Prestwich St ■ 061 434 0813 ■ RRR

Tucked away in the office district of Green Point, Beluga offers Eastern-influenced grills, seafood and excellent-value sushi.

7 Chef's Warehouse
MAP P4 ■ 92 Bree St ■ 021 422 0128 ■ RR

There are no reservations at this busy spot. Most people come for the ever-changing "tapas for two" option.

Tables at atmospheric Africa Café

8 Africa Café
MAP P4 ■ 108 Shortmarket St ■ 021 422 0221 ■ RRR

A nightly pan-African buffet makes this a great option for sampling the varied flavours of the continent.

9 Gold Restaurant
MAP P3 ■ 15 Bennett St ■ 021 421 4653 ■ RRR

Experience Gold's African 14-course tasting menu. In the evening there's traditional dancers, drumming, hand-washing and Mali puppets.

10 La Parada
MAP P5 ■ 107 Bree St ■ 021 426 0330 ■ RR

A popular spot on Bree Street, La Parada is renowned for its excellent tapas dishes such as crispy calamari and prawn croquettes. The bar serves delicious cocktails and craft beer.

Beef short ribs at La Parada

See map on p66–7

TOP 10 Southern Suburbs

Cape Town's most significant cluster of suburban attractions lies amidst a belt of leafy residential properties that stretches southward from the city centre, flanked to the west by Table Mountain and to the east by the incongruously poor Cape Flats. It's an area of interest for nature lovers, with both Kirstenbosch and Tokai offering scenic surroundings for a stroll. The estates along the Constantia Wine Route are as enjoyable as their more far-flung counterparts around Stellenbosch.

Grapes on a vine

1 Tokai Plantation and Arboretum

MAP H3 ■ Tokai Rd ■ Open Apr–Sep: 8am–5pm daily; Oct–Mar: 7am–6pm daily ■ Adm ■ www.sanparks.org

Set in Table Mountain National Park, this pine-tree plantation encloses a Victorian arboretum that is popular with bird-watchers. Its winged residents include the forest buzzard and Verreaux's eagle. The Plantation is a managed forest, and areas may be closed for harvesting.

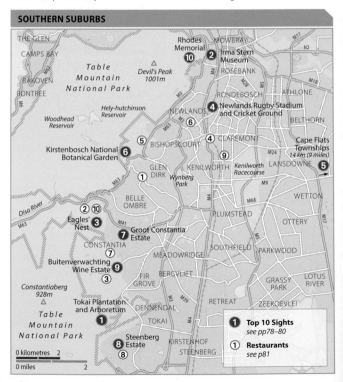

SOUTHERN SUBURBS

- 1 Top 10 Sights
  see pp78–80
- 1 Restaurants
  see p81

0 kilometres 2
0 miles 2

② Irma Stern Museum
MAP H1 ■ 21 Cecil Rd, Rosebank
■ 021 650 7240 ■ Open 10am–5pm
Tue–Fri, 10am–2pm Sat ■ Adm
■ www.irmasternmuseum.co.za

This underrated museum opened
in 1971 in the house where versatile
artist Irma Stern lived till her death
in 1966. Trained in Germany, Stern
gained international acclaim for
her impressionist portraits, but
her idealized rendition of African
subjects provoked controversy at
home. As well as her paintings,
the museum also houses Stern's
collection of Africana, notably an
early 20th-century Congolese stool.

③ Eagle's Nest
MAP H2 ■ Old Constantia
Main Rd, Constantia ■ 021 794 4095
■ Open 10am–4:30pm daily ■ Adm for
tasting ■ www.eaglesnestwines.com

One of Constantia's lesser-known
wineries, Eagle's Nest is a peaceful
and picturesque spot for a tasting –
the floral Viognier is one of their
most celebrated wines. Dining options
are simple, and in summer you can
enjoy a picnic in the leafy grounds.

④ Newlands Rugby Stadium and Cricket Ground
MAP H2

Newlands hosted its first international rugby test match in 1891.
A multipurpose venue with a crowd

Iconic sports venue Newlands

capacity of 51,900, it is home to one
of South Africa's Super Rugby teams
(see p54). Nearby, towering Table
Mountain looms over the scenic
Newlands Cricket Ground.

⑤ Cape Flats Townships
MAP C3, H1

Practically uninhabited until the
1940s, the sandy flats on the east of
the peninsula were urbanized after
the forced relocation of locals from
whites only suburbs to townships
such as Khayelitsha, Langa and
Gugulethu. Despite upliftment,
poverty is still high.

⑥ Kirstenbosch National Botanical Garden

This beautiful botanical garden *(see
pp26–7)* extends up to the eastern
slopes of Table Mountain. It has a rich
selection of flora and birdlife typical
to the Western Cape. The network of
footpaths, some suitable for wheelchair users, leads visitors onwards
and upwards to explore the *fynbos*-
draped slopes of Table Mountain.

**Magnificent Kirstenbosch
National Botanical Garden**

Rolling vineyards of the historic Groot Constantia Wine Estate

(7) Groot Constantia Wine Estate

South Africa's oldest wine estate *(see pp28–9)* is situated in the suburb of Constantia, below the eastern contours of Table Mountain. The opportunity to taste the award-winning wines alone justifies a visit, as does the stately Manor House.

(8) Steenberg Estate

MAP H3 ■ Steenberg Rd, Tokai ■ 021 713 2211 ■ Tasting 10am–6pm daily ■ www.steenbergfarm.com

Located on the oldest farm in the Constantia Valley, and set below the eponymous "Stone Mountain", Steenberg was established in 1682 as Swaaneweide by Catharina Ras. Its award-winning wines are headed by a superb Sauvignon Blanc reserve and a red blend bearing Catharina's name. The estate has a championship golf course *(see p54)*, a luxury hotel and two restaurants.

(9) Buitenverwachting Wine Estate

MAP H3 ■ 37 Klein Constantia Rd, Constantia ■ 021 794 5190 ■ Tasting 10am–4pm Mon–Sat ■ www.buiten verwachting.co.za

Translated as "Beyond Expectations" – an allusion to the 100-tonne grape harvest reaped by Ryk Cloete in 1825 – this 18th-century Cape Dutch homestead is set at the foot of Constantia Mountain. Though the flagship wine is a Bordeaux-style blend (Christine), the estate also produces unblended reds and whites.

(10) Rhodes Memorial

MAP H1 ■ 021 687 0000 ■ Restaurant: open 9am–5pm daily ■ www.rhodesmemorial.co.za

One-time prime minister of the Cape and founder of the Rhodesias (now Zimbabwe and Zambia), C J Rhodes has a memorial dedicated to him on a lookout point below Devil's Peak, which offers memorable views across the Cape Flats. Built in Neo-Classical style, the monument has Doric columns and stone lions modelled on Nelson's Column.

RHODES MEMORIAL CONTROVERSY

In 2015, an intruder defaced the Rhodes Memorial's bronze bust with graffiti denouncing its subject. This incident was sparked by the divisive #RhodesMustFall campaign, which argues that the removal of memorials to this poster boy of white supremacy and Victorian imperialism is a necessary step in the decolonization of African history. Detractors view it as historical revisionism; the controversy rages on.

Restaurants

PRICE CATEGORIES
For a three-course meal for one, including half a bottle of wine, cover charge, taxes and extra charges.

R under R300 **RR** R300–400 **RRR** over R400

1 Greenhouse
MAP H2 ■ 93 Brommersvlei Rd, Constantia ■ 021 795 6226 ■ RRR

Gorgeous fusion cuisine is served at this stylish restaurant in The Cellars-Hohenort hotel (see p116).

2 Chef's Warehouse at Beau Constantia
MAP H2 ■ 1043 Constantia Main Rd ■ 021 794 8632 ■ RR

A sister restaurant of Chef's Warehouse (see p77), this place serves excellent tapas and affords stunning views of the Constantia Valley.

3 Beyond Restaurant
MAP H2 ■ Buitenverwachting, 37 Klein Constantia Rd ■ 021 794 5190 ■ RRR

Set in a Cape Dutch building, this Buitenverwachting Estate restaurant combines continental and local influences. There is also a café, Coffee BloC.

4 A Tavola
MAP H2 ■ Wilderness Rd, Claremont ■ 021 671 1763 ■ RR

A rather humdrum location, but the authentic Italian food amply compensates. From a terrace table you can glimpse Table Mountain.

5 Moyo Kirstenbosch
In Kirstenbosch National Botanical Garden (see pp26–7), Moyo's menu includes filled pancakes, sandwiches and picnic baskets.

6 Vineyard Hotel
MAP H2 ■ 60 Colinton Rd, Newlands ■ 021 657 4500 ■ RRR

Lunch outdoors in the leafy gardens of the Vineyard Hotel (see p116), or indoors in the Art Deco-inspired restaurant. The food is a fusion of eastern and western cuisine – try the seven-course tasting menu with wine pairings.

7 Jonkershuis Restaurant
MAP H2 ■ Groot Constantia Wine Estate ■ 021 794 6255 ■ RR

This pleasant restaurant, set on the historic Groot Constantia Wine Estate, offers a hearty Cape Malay menu. Lunch is best enjoyed at outdoor tables under the giant oaks.

Chic setting at Bistro Sixteen82

8 Bistro Sixteen82
MAP H3 ■ Steenberg Estate, Tokai ■ 021 713 2211 ■ RR

The bistro and tapas menu raises the standard of casual dining to an art form without the prices to match.

9 Banana Jam Café
MAP H2 ■ 157 2nd Ave, Kenilworth ■ 021 674 0186 ■ R

This colourful restaurant serves good-value pizza and burgers, plus Caribbean dishes. There's a brewpub upstairs with 30 local beers on tap, and a vast collection of rums from the Caribbean islands.

10 La Colombe
MAP H2 ■ Silvermist Wine Estate, Constantia ■ 021 794 2390 ■ RRR

Perched on the side of a mountain with views over the Constantia Valley, this relaxed yet ultra-elegant spot serves contemporary cuisine fusing local ingredients with French flair.

See map on p78

TOP 10 The Cape Peninsula

The Cape Peninsula is a mountainous sliver of land that extends southward from Cape Town to Cape Point, and is flanked by the open Atlantic to the west and False Bay to the east. Two-thirds of the coastline along the north of the peninsula are studded with quaint villages, sandy beaches and pretty seaside resorts. In the south, the ragged mountain spine supports a cover of unspoilt *fynbos* interspersed with plantation forest. Most of the peninsula is protected within Table Mountain National Park (TMNP). Visitors could spend a lifetime exploring it, but highlights include the Cape of Good Hope, the penguin colony at Boulders Beach near Simon's Town, and lovely beaches at Muizenberg, Noordhoek and Fish Hoek.

Night heron in the Rondevlei Bird Sanctuary

THE CAPE PENINSULA

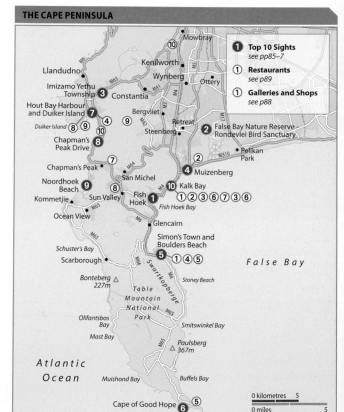

- **1** Top 10 Sights
  see pp85–7
- **1** Restaurants
  see p89
- **1** Galleries and Shops
  see p88

Previous pages Buitenverwachting Wine Estate, set against Constantia Mountain

The village of Fish Hoek and its magnificent beach

1 Fish Hoek
MAP H4

The quaint village of Fish Hoek lies at the mouth of the Silvermine River between Muizenberg and Simon's Town, and boasts one of the warmest and safest swimming beaches on the Peninsula. The clifftop Jager's Path offers good vantage points for whale watching. Overlooking the town is Peers Cave, one of the Cape's most important archaeological sites, which contains evidence of human occupation dating back 11,000 years.

2 False Bay Nature Reserve - Rondevlei Bird Sanctuary
MAP H3 ■ Perth Rd, Rondevlei ■ 021 706 2404 ■ Open 7:30am–5pm daily; Dec–Feb: 7:30am–5pm Mon–Fri, 7:30am–7pm Sat & Sun ■ Adm

A short drive north of Muizenberg, Cape Town's best bird sanctuary is home to around 230 species, which can be glimpsed from the short walking trails that connect the viewing towers and bird hides. Grebes, rails, herons, ibises, pelicans and gulls are represented here. Hippos were introduced in 1982 to control the spread of surface vegetation.

3 Imizamo Yethu Township
MAP G2 ■ City Sightseeing: 021 511 6000; tours 10:30am–4pm daily ■ Adm ■ www.citysightseeing.co.za

An isiXhosa phrase meaning "Our Efforts", this township was established on the outskirts of Hout Bay after the collapse of apartheid in the 1990s. It grew rapidly and is now a community of around 34,000 people living in rudimentary houses. Forty-minute guided walks of IY (the local name for the township) are offered by the City Sightseeing Bus.

4 Muizenberg
MAP H3

This resort town on False Bay was the location chosen a century ago by Witwatersrand gold magnates to build a row of seafront mansions. Historical sights include Het Posthuys, built as a tollhouse in 1742, battlements that are remnants of the 1795 Anglo-Dutch Battle of Muizenberg, the Edwardian railway station and Rhodes Cottage Museum, where C J Rhodes died in 1902. The wide, sheltered beach is a real haven for surfers and swimmers.

Colourful huts on Muizenberg beach

Penguin colony at Boulders Beach

5 Simon's Town and Boulders Beach

A naval base for over 200 years, the pleasantly time-warped Simon's Town *(see pp30–31)* is enhanced by the "Historic Mile", a row of Victorian façades lining St George's Street. The Victorian railway station is the southern terminus of one of the world's great suburban train rides, following the False Bay seafront to Muizenberg. The penguin colony south of town at Boulders Beach is the main attraction.

6 Cape of Good Hope

This reserve *(see pp32–3)* is the scenic highlight of the peninsula, dotted with stunning viewpoints such as Rooikrans, Gifkommetjie and Cape Point. It is a key stronghold for the Cape's unique *fynbos* habitat and for wildlife such as the eland and the endemic bontebok.

Cape of Good Hope's rugged point

7 Hout Bay Harbour and Duiker Island
MAP G3 ■ Hout Bay ■ Tours hourly

Hout Bay's busy little harbour is the launching point for boat trips to Duiker Island, a flat granite outcrop that lies about 6 km (4 miles) offshore. The island's rocky shores support 5,000–6,000 Cape fur seals. People are forbidden from landing on the island, but plenty of seals can be seen from the boats, which also have windows for underwater viewing. Various marine birds including black oystercatchers, African penguins and breeding colonies of three different cormorant species may also be spotted here.

Vertiginous Chapman's Peak Drive

8 Chapman's Peak Drive
MAP G3 ■ Adm for vehicles
■ www.chapmanspeakdrive.co.za

Named after the peak that soars above it, Chapman's Peak Drive, constructed in 1915–22, is a stunning stretch of road. Set into an almost-vertical cliff face that connects Hout Bay to Noordhoek, the drive offers great viewing points and is now a toll road after years of repair work.

CAPE FLORAL KINGDOM

The smallest of the world's six floral kingdoms, the Cape consists of a unique floral community known as *fynbos* (fine bush), a reference to the narrow leaves of many plants. A UNESCO World Heritage Site and a biodiversity hotspot for its floral wealth, the Cape Peninsula supports almost 20 per cent of Africa's flora – home to an estimated 9,000 plant species.

⑨ Noordhoek Beach
MAP G3

An expanse of bone-white sand running from the base of Chapman's Peak to Kommetjie, Noordhoek is the most beautiful beach on the Cape Peninsula. It is a lovely spot for walks and bird-watching; visitors may even catch a glimpse of the endangered black oystercatcher. Horse riding is also on offer here *(see p54)*.

⑩ Kalk Bay
MAP H3

This artsy seaside suburb has plenty to keep its visitors occupied. The Olympia Café *(see p89)* is a favourite breakfast haunt, where you can fuel up for a day browsing the many galleries, boutiques and antiques shops lining Main Road *(see p88)*. Restaurants specializing in seafood line the waterfront, and you can wander the pier watching the busy fisherman bringing in their latest catch. Keep an eye out for the seals that climb up onto the harbour in search of fishy morsels, much to the fishmongers' dismay.

A FULL-DAY DRIVING TOUR TO CAPE POINT

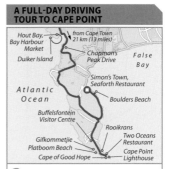

▶ MORNING

After an early breakfast, head down to the Atlantic Seaboard via Camps Bay to **Hout Bay**. Once there, go on the 40-minute boat excursion to see the seals on **Duiker Island**, and, if it's the weekend, pop into **Bay Harbour Market** *(see p88)*. Then continue your journey with stops along **Chapman's Peak Drive** to enjoy the view, driving south to the **Cape of Good Hope** sector of Table Mountain National Park *(see p45)*. Stop at the **Buffelsfontein Visitor Centre** before you reach the Cape Point car park. If you're already peckish, enjoy a scenic lunch at the **Two Oceans Restaurant** *(see p89)* overlooking False Bay, or wait until after you've climbed the steep footpath (or caught the funicular) to **Cape Point Lighthouse** *(see p33)*.

AFTERNOON

Walk off the lunch following the footpath from the Cape of Good Hope Beach, or drive back along the main road through the reserve towards the entrance gate, diverting to the **Rooikrans**, **Gifkommetjie** or **Platboom Beach**. Leave by 3pm, following the road that hugs the False Bay coast towards **Simon's Town**. Stop occasionally to look out for whales. Before you reach Simon's Town, turn right for **Boulders Beach** to watch the squabbling penguins. Before driving back, enjoy a coffee at **Seaforth Restaurant** *(see p89)*, overlooking the harbour in Simon's Town.

See map on p84 ←

Galleries and Shops

1 Kalk Bay Artists Studio and Gallery
MAP H3 ▪ 136 Main Rd, Kalk Bay
▪ 076 246 0728

Situated in the Olympia Building, the gallery features abstract art of Christine Crowley and experimental work of Anastasia Sarantinou.

2 Artvark Gallery
MAP H3 ▪ 48 Main Rd, Kalk Bay ▪ 021 788 5584

A contemporary gallery showcasing South African art and crafts, plus custom and exclusive steelworks.

3 Kalk Bay Modern
MAP H3 ▪ 136 Main Rd, Kalk Bay ▪ 021 788 6571

Also located in the Olympia Building, this art gallery features a large collection of contemporary San art.

4 Rockchic
35 Main Rd, Hout Bay ▪ 021 791 4162

This friendly little shop specializes in chunky jewellery, handmade with semi-precious gems and beads.

5 Quayside Centre
MAP H4 ▪ Simon's Town

Below the Quayside Hotel *(see p116)*, this complex has a range of curio shops, an art gallery and places to eat overlooking Simon's Town's harbour.

Quagga Rare Books & Art

6 Quagga Rare Books & Art
MAP H3 ▪ 86 Main Rd, Kalk Bay ▪ 021 788 2752

This highly regarded bookshop has numerous antiquarian titles.

7 Papagayo
MAP H3 ▪ 1 Belmont Rd, Kalk Bay ▪ 021 788 1923

Bargains can be found at this large warehouse piled high with handicrafts, textiles, clothing and decor items.

8 Longbeach Mall
MAP G3 ▪ Buller Louw Blvd, Sunnydale ▪ 021 785 5955

The southern peninsula's largest shopping centre contains more than 100 shops and leisure venues including supermarkets, a craft market, restaurants and cafés.

9 Bay Harbour Market
MAP G2 ▪ 31 Harbour Rd, Hout Bay ▪ 084 370 5715 ▪ Open 5–9pm Fri, 9:30am–4pm Sat & Sun

Filled with craft stalls, quirky clothes and lots of good food, this is one of Cape Town's best markets.

10 Montebello Design Centre
MAP H2 ▪ 31 Newlands Ave, Newlands ▪ 021 685 6445

Housed in restored farm buildings, this centre has over 20 art and crafts studios and workshops, a restaurant and an organic deli and farm shop.

Stalls at Quayside Centre

Restaurants

1 **Lighthouse Café**
MAP H4 ■ 90 St Georges St, Simon's Town ■ 021 786 9000 ■ R
It doesn't boast the location that some Simon's Town restaurants have, but the friendly atmosphere and honest, affordable food more than make up for there being a road between you and the ocean.

2 **Tiger's Milk**
MAP H3 ■ Beach Rd, Muizenberg ■ 021 788 1860 ■ RR
Grab a spot by the huge, ocean-facing windows and enjoy local craft beer with a pizza, burger or "bunny chow", a local speciality consisting of curry in a hollowed-out loaf of bread.

3 **Harbour House**
MAP H3 ■ Kalk Bay Harbour ■ 021 788 4136 ■ RRR
This upstairs restaurant is as close to the ocean as you can get inside Kalk Bay Harbour, with huge glass windows looking out onto the ocean. It offers understated fine dining.

Harbour House's ocean view

4 **Seaforth Restaurant**
MAP H4 ■ Seaforth Beach, Simon's Town ■ 021 786 4810 ■ RR
This seafood restaurant serves excellent pasta and pizza. Combine with a visit to the penguins (see p86).

5 **Two Oceans Restaurant and Snack Bar**
MAP H6 ■ Cape Point ■ 021 780 9200 ■ Closed for dinner ■ RRR
Famed for its fine Cape seafood and sublime sushi, this first-rate

PRICE CATEGORIES
For a three-course meal for one, including half a bottle of wine, cover charge, taxes and extra charges.

R under R300 **RR** R300–400 **RRR** over R400

restaurant at Cape Point is also known for its truly staggering views across False Bay.

6 **Olympia Café**
MAP H3 ■ 134 Main Rd, Kalk Bay ■ 021 788 6396 ■ RR
People queue here for the laid-back seaside atmosphere, excellent breakfasts and Mediterranean dishes.

7 **The Foodbarn**
MAP G3 ■ Noordhoek Farm Village, Village Lane, Noordhoek ■ 021 789 1390 ■ RRR
Chef Franck Dangereux is a master of taste and flavour. The restaurant reflects French gastronomy, while the deli serves light meals and takeaway pies and quiches.

8 **Wharfside Grill Restaurant**
MAP G2 ■ Harbour Rd, Hout Bay ■ 021 790 1100 ■ RRR
Located in the Mariner's Wharf, this nautical-themed restaurant serves fresh seafood. The Wharfette Bistro downstairs sells reasonably priced takeaway fish and chips.

9 **Dunes**
MAP G2 ■ 1 Beach Rd, Hout Bay ■ 021 790 1876 ■ RR
On the sands of Hout Bay beach, this bistro serves tapas, salads, seafood, steaks and pizzas. It's good for families, and has a children's playground.

10 **Chefs Warehouse at Tintswalo Atlantic**
MAP G3 ■ Chapman's Peak Drive ■ 021 541 0165 ■ RRR
This fine-dining restaurant has a stunning location on the Atlantic seaboard. Reservations are essential.

See map on p84

🔟 The Winelands

The mountainous territory immediately inland of Cape Town, often referred to as the Boland (literally "Uplands"), is among the most beautiful parts of South Africa, and is dotted with lush, well-watered valleys amongst its rugged sandstone peaks. This region also forms the heart of the country's wine industry, and is home to around 300 wineries. The Winelands' historic towns include Stellenbosch, Franschhoek, Tulbagh and Paarl.

Climbing in the Jonkershoek

1 Jonkershoek Nature Reserve

MAP E3 ■ 021 483 0190 (Jonkershoek Valley) ■ Jonkershoek Valley and Assegaaibosch: open Apr–Oct: 8am–6pm daily; Nov–Mar: 8am–7pm daily ■ Adm ■ www.capenature.co.za

This mountainous reserve on the outskirts of Stellenbosch is

THE WINELANDS

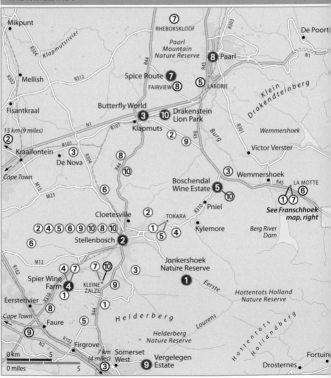

Historic winery at Stellenbosch

traversed by hiking trails, ranging from easy paths through the farmland of the Assegaaibosch sector to the demanding hikes to the upper slopes. The mountain scenery hosts more than 1,100 species of *fynbos* plants and a wide range of birds. The large mammal population includes leopards, baboons and klipspringers.

Franschhoek

2 Stellenbosch

The tourist capital of the Winelands lies amid mountainous surrounds on the banks of the Eerste River. Established just 27 years after Cape Town was settled, Stellenbosch *(see pp34–5)* is South Africa's second-oldest town and boasts the country's highest concentration of pre-20th-century Cape Dutch buildings. Despite its historic feel, Stellenbosch is anything but staid, thanks partly to the bustling student life associated with its university. The compact town centre is lively – and very safe – even after dark.

3 Butterfly World

MAP D1 ▪ R44, Klapmuts ▪ 062 879 4044 ▪ Open 9am–4:30pm daily ▪ Adm ▪ www.butterflyworld.co.za

Butterfly World is South Africa's largest butterfly park and supports more than 20 indigenous free-flying species in an attractive, landscaped indoor garden. It is also home to small antelopes and iguanas, as well as tarantulas and other spiders in terrariums. There's a tea garden, a picnic area and a craft shop on site.

Idia butterfly at Butterfly World

CAPE DUTCH HOUSES

Cape Dutch architecture evolved in the 18th century, adapting European styles to suit African conditions. Its defining feature, derived from medieval houses in Amsterdam, is an ornate round gable above the entrance. Typical buildings, such as the manor at Vergelegen, have a thatched roof and a H-shaped floorplan.

4 Spier Wine Farm
MAP D3 ▪ Off R310 en route Stellenbosch ▪ 021 809 1143 ▪ Tasting 9am–5pm Mon–Thu, 9am–7:30pm Fri–Sun ▪ Adm ▪ www.spier.co.za

This beautiful estate is one of South Africa's oldest wine farms. The sophisticated wine-tasting venue, on the banks of the Spier Dam, pairs Spier signature wines with innovative food and also offers a children's grape juice tasting menu. The estate has a picnic hamper service, the Eight Restaurant, a spa, a playground, a craft market, Eagle Encounter shows and the superb Spier Hotel (see p117), with its impressive and modern decor.

Boschendal Wine Estate

5 Boschendal Wine Estate
The Boschendal Estate (see p36) was first planted with vines by Huguenot settler Jean de Long in 1685. Set in a green valley flanked by the Groot Drakenstein and Simonsberg Mountains, the estate is reached via a tree-lined drive. The Cape Dutch architecture here includes a manor house dating to 1812 and a cellar built in 1795. There is a restaurant and café, but, on fine days, a sumptuous picnic on the lawns is irresistible.

6 Franschhoek
MAP F2

Franschhoek (see pp36–7) is the self-styled culinary capital of South Africa. With a French influence that dates back to its settlement by Huguenot refugees in the late 17th century, its history is documented in the Huguenot Memorial Museum. Many wineries are to be found nearby, and stylish shops and world-class restaurants line the main street.

7 Spice Route
MAP E1 ▪ Suid Agter Paarl Rd, Paarl ▪ 021 863 5200 ▪ Open 9am–5pm daily ▪ www.spiceroute.co.za

At this artisans' village, everything is brewed, distilled, cured, baked or fermented on site. Join a chocolate tasting, learn how charcuterie is produced, taste outstanding wines, visit the microbrewery, and finish your day with food ranging from wood-fired pizza to spice-rubbed steak.

8 Paarl
MAP E1 ▪ 021 872 4842 ▪ www.paarl online.com

Hemmed in by Paarl Mountain to the west and the Berg River to the east, the largest town in the Winelands is a bit scruffy compared to Stellenbosch. Paarl Mountain, a granite outcrop in a nature reserve, and the Afrikaans Language Monument are worth a visit, and the Laborie Wine Estate is charming.

The Afrikaans Language Monument, Paarl

Garden walkway at Vergelegen

9 Vergelegen Estate

MAP E4 ■ Lourensford Rd, Somerset West ■ 021 847 2100 ■ Open 8:30am–5pm (last entry 4pm) daily ■ Adm ■ www.vergelegen.co.za

Translated as "lying afar", this historic property on the slopes of the Helderberg started life as a remote outpost of the Cape Colony in 1685. Fifteen years later, it became the private estate of Willem van der Stel, who established the elegant manor house and octagonal garden, and planted the gnarled camphor trees at its entrance. This is one of South Africa's premier estates for its magnificent grounds and range of wines, and it is well worth making the journey here.

10 Drakenstein Lion Park

MAP E1 ■ Old Paarl Rd (R101), Klapmuts ■ 021 863 3290 ■ Open 9am–5pm daily ■ Adm ■ www.lionrescue.org.za

This park, founded in 1998, provides lifelong sanctuary to captive-born big cats that have been abused or suffered distress and would not be able, because of their upbringing, to fend for themselves in the wild. More than 30 of these magnificent animals live freely and safely in over 20 ha (50 acres) of natural habitat. The highlight of a visit is to sleep overnight in the Ingonyama Tented Camp set within the lions' territory.

THE "FOUR PASSES" DAY CIRCUIT

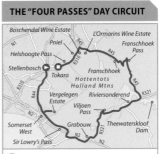

▶ MORNING

The circuit around the **Hottentots Holland Mountains** encompasses some of the Winelands' finest scenery, architecture and wine estates. Starting in **Stellenbosch** (see pp34–5), drive south along the R44 towards **Somerset West**. Follow the signs for the **Vergelegen Estate** on the Helderberg slopes. Once here, explore the historic buildings and pause for a coffee or a wine tasting. From Somerset West, follow the N2 east via **Sir Lowry's Pass**, then turn left onto the R321, passing through **Grabouw** and over **Viljoen Pass** before descending into the **Riviersonderend** "River Without End" Valley to **Theewaterskloof Dam**. Turn left onto the R45, which traverses the **Franschhoek Pass**, offering wonderful views over the town whose name it bears.

AFTERNOON

In **Franschhoek**, cruise the main road to choose a lunch spot from one of the many excellent dining establishments. Then pop into the Huguenot Memorial and Museum (see p37) or browse the shops along the main street. Continue west along the R45 and stop at **L'Ormarins Wine Estate** to visit the Franschhoek Motor Museum (see p36). Outside Franschhoek, branch left onto the R310 to reach Stellenbosch via the **Helshoogte Pass**. Stop en route at the **Boschendal Wine Estate**, the town of **Pniel** and Hillcrest Berries Farm. End your day with a drink at the **Tokara** estate's restaurant (see p95).

See map on pp90–91 ←

Galleries and Shops

1 Root 44 Market
MAP D3 ■ Audacia Wines, R44/Annandale Rd, Stellenbosch ■ 021 300 3935

This lively market is one of the Winelands' finest. Open every weekend, it's not just a place to shop for crafts and organic food – you can have lunch, taste beer and wine, and listen to live music while the kids enjoy the playground.

2 Oom Samie Se Winkel
MAP D2 ■ 84 Dorp St, Stellenbosch ■ 021 887 0797

Stellenbosch's most famous *winkel* (shop) is over 100 years old and retains a Victorian appearance. It features an eclectic range of affordable local craftwork and genuine Africana.

3 The Ceramics Gallery
MAP F2 ■ 24 Dirkie Uys St, Franschhoek ■ 021 876 4304

View beautiful, utilitarian pottery by David Walters and even watch him working at the wheel.

Karoo Classics' elegant leather goods

4 Karoo Classics
MAP D2 ■ De Wet Centre, Church St, Stellenbosch ■ 071 606 1869

Handcrafted accessories made of the softest mohair, local ostrich leather and other natural, regional materials are the speciality at this shop in Stellenbosch's town centre.

5 Local Works
MAP D2 ■ 10 Drostdy St, Stellenbosch ■ 021 887 0875

This impressive little shop supports local artists and has a collection of handpicked pieces that highlight the diversity of African art and culture.

6 Is Art Stellenbosch
MAP F2 ■ 29 Church St, Stellenbosch ■ 021 883 9717

Named after owner Ilse Schermers Griesel, this vibrant gallery showcases contemporary South African art as well as local antiques and collectables.

7 Huguenot Fine Chocolates
MAP F2 ■ 1 Daniel Hugo St, Franschhoek ■ 021 876 4096

Delicious chocolates created by two local Belgian-trained chocolatiers are sold at this popular boutique.

Root 44 Market

8 Vineyard Connection
MAP D2 ■ Delvera Farm, Cnr R44 & Muldersvlei Rd, Stellenbosch ■ 081 458 7804

This shop, located between Paarl and Stellenbosch, stocks the Cape's finest wines and can ship overseas.

9 Stellenbosch University Museum
MAP D2 ■ 52 Ryneveld St, Stellenbosch ■ 021 808 3695 ■ Open 9am–4:30pm Mon–Sat

This tiered, Neo-Classical building displays the university's collection of 19th- and 20th-century art, and an anthropological collection of traditional African crafts and household objects.

10 Rupert Museum
A superb collection of contemporary South African art amassed by Dr Anton Rupert is housed in this gallery (see p35).

Wine Estates Near Stellenbosch

1 Seven Sisters Vineyard
MAP D3 ▪ Annandale Rd,
Stellenbosch ▪ 021 879 1996
▪ Open 9am–4pm Mon–Sat, tasting
by appt ▪ www.sevensisters.co.za
Established in 2005 by seven sisters,
this inspiring winery brings a personal
touch to its range of whites and reds.

2 Rustenberg Wines
MAP E2 ▪ Rustenberg Rd ▪ 021
809 1200 ▪ Tasting 10am–4:30pm
Mon–Fri, 10am–4pm Sat, 10am–3pm
Sun ▪ www.rustenberg.co.za
This 300-year-old farm is known
for its crisp Chardonnays.

3 Villiera
MAP D3 ▪ R304 ▪ 021 865
2002 ▪ Open 9am–5pm Mon–Fri,
9am–3pm Sat ▪ www.villiera.com
Before you try a tasting of MCC
(Méthode Cap Classique), you can
join a guided game drive to see
zebra, giraffe and a host of antelope.

4 Delaire Graff
A "vineyard in the sky" on the
crest of Helshoogte Pass, Delaire Graff
(see p36) makes good reds, and its
grounds are perfect for picnics.

5 Tokara
Located on Helshoogte Pass,
Tokara *(see p36)* has a scenically
positioned restaurant. As well as
its acclaimed wines, it is renowned
for its superb olive oil.

Vineyard views for diners at Tokara

6 Simonsig
MAP D2 ▪ Kromm Rhee Rd
▪ 021 888 4900 ▪ Open 10am–4pm
Sat–Wed, 10am–6pm Thu & Fri
▪ www.simonsig.co.za
South Africa's first producer of MCC
offers an excellent, free cellar tour
explaining the process. Tours end
with a demonstration of the *sabrage* –
opening a bottle with a sword.

7 Spier Wine Farm
This estate *(see p92)* has
mid-priced, very quaffable wines
and lots of family-oriented activities.

8 Meerlust
MAP D3 ▪ R310 ▪ 021 843 3587
▪ Tasting 9am–5pm Mon–Fri, 10am–
2pm Sat ▪ www.meerlust.co.za
At Meerlust, the cellar is stocked with
the iconic claret-style Rubicon blend.

9 Blaauwklippen
MAP D3 ▪ R44 ▪ 021 880
0133 ▪ Open 10am–6pm Wed–Sun
▪ www.blaauwklippen.com
Founded in 1682, this estate is one of
Stellenbosch's oldest. It offers quaility
Zinfandel and is home to a manor
and a bistro. The Sunday market has
craft stalls and activities for children.

10 Kanonkop
MAP D2 ▪ R44 ▪ 021 884 4656
▪ Tasting 9am–5pm Mon–Fri, 9am–
2pm Sat ▪ www.kanonkop.co.za
As well as several award-winning
blends, Kanonkop also produces one
of South Africa's finest Pinotages.

Other Wine Estates

La Motte's tasting room

1 La Motte
MAP F2 ▪ R45 Main Rd, Franschhoek ▪ 021 876 8000 ▪ Tasting 9am–5pm Tue–Sat (from 11am Tue) ▪ www.la-motte.com
Award-winning wines in a lovely spot (see p37) in the Franschhoek Valley.

2 Durbanville Hills
MAP C2 ▪ M13, Tygervalley Rd ▪ 021 558 1300 ▪ Tasting noon–6pm Mon, 10am–6pm Tue–Fri, 10am–5pm Sat, 11am–5pm Sun ▪ www.durban villehills.co.za
Visit the Durbanville Hills estate for some excellent plummy Merlots.

3 Waterkloof
MAP D4 ▪ Sir Lowry's Pass Rd, Somerset West ▪ 021 858 1292 ▪ Tasting 10am–4:30pm Wed–Sun ▪ www.waterkloofwines.co.za
Set in a space-age glass box perched on a slope, Waterkloof's tasting lounge and restaurant have incredible views of False Bay, the Hottentots Holland and Helderberg mountains. The estate is known for its elegant wines.

4 Haute Cabrière
MAP F2 ▪ Franschhoek Pass Rd ▪ 021 876 2630 ▪ Tasting: 10am–5pm Mon–Fri, 10am–6:30pm Sat, 10am–3pm Sun; cellar tours: by appt ▪ www.cabriere.co.za
Haute Cabrière produces world-class sparkling wines. The corks are removed with a sword.

5 Laborie
MAP E1 ▪ Taillefer St, Paarl ▪ 021 807 3095 ▪ Tasting 11am–4pm daily ▪ www.laborieestate.co.za
Located in Paarl since 1698, Laborie is famous for its Chardonnay, Pinot Noir and Méthode Cap Classique.

6 Leopard's Leap
MAP F2 ▪ R45 Main Rd, Franschhoek ▪ 021 876 8002 ▪ Tasting 9am–5pm Tue–Sat, 11am–5pm Sun ▪ www.leopardsleap.co.za
This modern tasting room, with elements of wood, glass and chrome, has a colouful range of wine cocktails.

7 Rhebokskloof
MAP E1 ▪ Windmeul, Agter Paarl ▪ 021 869 8386 ▪ Tasting 9am–5pm daily ▪ www.rhebokskloof.co.za
Encircled by mountains, this estate offers leisure and adventure activities.

8 Fairview
MAP E1 ▪ Suid-Agter Paarl Rd ▪ 021 863 2450 ▪ Tasting 9am–5pm daily ▪ www.fairview.co.za
A popular estate, Fairview produces fine wines and has a superb deli that serves handcrafted goat's cheese.

9 Vergenoegd
MAP D3 ▪ Baden Powell Dr, R310, Stellenbosch ▪ 021 843 3248 ▪ Tasting 8am–4pm Mon–Sat ▪ www.vergenoegd.co.za
This estate features a wine-blending experience, cellar tours and picnics. Children will enjoy the large flock of Indian runner ducks. Reservations are necessary.

10 Kleine Zalze
MAP D3 ▪ R44, Stellenbosch ▪ 021 880 0717 ▪ Tasting 9am–6pm Mon–Sat, 11am–6pm Sun ▪ www.kleinezalze.co.za
Best known for its restaurant Kleine Zalze (see p98), this estate also has a golf course and guest rooms (see p117).

Iconic Wines

 Kanonkop Paul Sauer
This is one of South Africa's most celebrated Bordeaux blends, led always by Cabernet Sauvignon. It has a restrained style, and is medium-bodied with a very well-judged level of oak.

2 Boekenhoutskloof Syrah
Marc Kent's reputation in the wine industry was established in 1997 when he produced this wine with his first harvest. Now an industry benchmark, it leans towards Old World styling, but the taste is proudly individual.

3 Beyerskloof Pinotage Reserve
Made from South Africa's "own" grape, this wine was created in the early 1920s by crossing Pinot Noir with Cinsaut (known as Hermitage). Beyers Truter's name is synonymous with Pinotage, and this is a particularly good one.

4 Hamilton Russell Vineyards Pinot Noir
This Hemel-en-Aarde Valley property pioneered Pinot Noir in South Africa in the 1970s. Juxtaposing power and restraint, the wine's typical raspberry/cherry core is always well wrapped in assertive yet controlled tannins.

5 Beaumont Hope Marguerite Chenin Blanc
Chenin Blanc is the South African wine industry's workhorse, and finds its way into sparkling wines, dry table wines, sweet wines and brandy. This wine is smooth and fruitful but serious, with reined-in oaking.

6 Ken Forrester The FMC Chenin Blanc
As extravagant and outgoing a Chenin Blanc as Ken Forrester himself, this wine is individualistic, complex and sweet when it first hits the palate but with enough tang to finish long and dry.

7 Graham Beck Cuvée Clive
Produced only when the vintage is particularly fine, Cuvée Clive is the most prestigious Cap Classique méthode champenoise wine from an estate famed for its bubbly.

8 Nederburg Edelkeur Noble Late Harvest
The first Cape Noble Late Harvest (always made from Chenin Blanc), this wine exudes melon and apricot flavours, while limey acidity seams the sweetness and converts it into delicious nectar.

9 Meerlust Rubicon
A true icon, established in 1693 and owned by the Myburgh family since 1756, this is one of South Africa's first and best-known Bordeaux blends, with several prestigious awards to its name.

Tasting bar at Meerlust Estate

10 Cape Point Isliedh
With vineyards located right in the teeth of the Cape's notorious wind, where only white grapes can reach full ripeness, this is a white Bordeaux blend in which Sauvignon Blanc's stone fruit and herbs are enhanced by Sémillon and a touch of new oak. It benefits from long cellaring.

See map on pp90–91

Restaurants Around Stellenbosch

1 Tokara Delicatessen
MAP E2 ■ Helshoogte Pass
■ 021 808 5950 ■ Closed dinner ■ R
Created with Tokara's wide range of artisanal produce, this delicatessen offers healthy, good-value fare, and is great for weekend brunch. For fine dining try Tokara Restaurant.

Delicatessen at Tokara

2 Glen Carlou
MAP E2 ■ R45/Simondium Rd, Klapmuts ■ 021 875 5528 ■ Closed dinner ■ RRR
Based in the tasting room of the Glen Carlou Winery, this restaurant delivers perfectly presented plates of food with equally delicious views.

3 Majeka Kitchen
MAP D3 ■ 26–32 Houtkapper St, Stellenbosch ■ 021 880 1549 ■ Closed lunch ■ RRR
The restaurant at the Majeka House boutique hotel is renowned for serving cuisine that showcases local specialities.

4 Vadas Smokehouse
MAP D3 ■ Spier Wine Farm, R310, Stellenbosch ■ 021 809 1137 ■ Closed Mon ■ RR
Boasting an open-plan kitchen and garden tables, Vadas serves fresh local produce. Smoked meat dishes are the speciality, but the vegetarian selection is also good.

Dish at Babel at Babylonstoren

5 96 Winery Road
MAP D3 ■ Winery Rd (off R44), Somerset West ■ 021 842 2020 ■ RR
This country-style place has a changing menu of seasonal dishes. It also has a private cellar packed full of vintage Cape reds.

6 Jordan Restaurant
MAP D3 ■ Jordan Wine Estate, Stellenbosch Kloof Rd (off M12) ■ 021 881 3612 ■ RRR
The flavours of the locally sourced food at Jordan (see p59) are intense, as are the fabulous vineyard views.

7 Kleine Zalze Restaurant
MAP D3 ■ Kleine Zalze Wine Estate, R44, Stellenbosch ■ 021 880 8167 ■ Closed Mon ■ RRR
Formerly Terroir (see p58), this restaurant offers a changing selection of plats du jour reflecting local availability as well as a good tapas menu.

8 Helena's Restaurant
MAP D2 ■ 33 Church St, Stellenbosch ■ 021 883 8207 ■ RRR
Set in Coopmanhuijs Boutique Hotel (see p117), Helena's serves delicious dishes using local ingredients.

9 Babel Restaurant
MAP E2 ■ Babylonstoren Estate, Klapmuts-Simondium Rd, Klapmuts ■ 021 863 3852 ■ RRR
The menu here is simple and reflects the tastes of the season. Booking is essential.

10 Jardine Food & Wine Bar
MAP D2 ■ 1 Andringa St, Stellenbosch ■ 021 886 5020 ■ Closed Sun & Mon ■ RRR
A small but superb restaurant. The menu changes regularly, but the food is consistently excellent.

Restaurants Around Franschhoek

1 La Petite Colombe
MAP F2 ■ Leeu Estates, Dassenberg Rd, Franschhoek ■ 021 202 3395 ■ Closed lunch ■ RRR

A sister restaurant of the award-winning La Colombe in Constantia, La Petite Colombe (see p58) has imaginative five- or nine-course menus that display the local flavours.

2 Reuben's Restaurant and Bar
MAP F2 ■ 2 Daniel Hugo St, Franschhoek ■ 021 876 3772 ■ RRR

The brainchild of celebrity chef Reuben Riffel, this restaurant has an innovative brasserie-style menu with African, Asian and European influences.

3 Fyndraai
MAP E2 ■ Solms-Delta Wine Estate, off R45, Groot Drakenstein ■ 066 200 9397 ■ Closed dinner ■ RRR

Well known for its modern take on traditional Cape cuisine, the menu here explores the culinary heritage of the area.

4 Haute Cabrière Restaurant & Terrace
MAP F2 ■ Franschhoek Pass Rd, Franschhoek ■ 021 876 8500 ■ RRR

Offering stunning views from a 17th-century wine estate (see p96), this restaurant serves French and South African contemporary dishes.

5 Foliage
MAP F2 ■ 11 Huguenot St ■ 021 876 2328 ■ Closed Sun ■ RRR

The menu here changes seasonally and features dishes made with free range and organic ingredients.

6 La Petite Ferme
MAP F2 ■ Franschhoek Pass Rd, Franschhoek ■ 021 876 3016 ■ Closed dinner Sun–Thu ■ RRR

A glass veranda offers views over the Franschhoek Valley, and the global menu does the location full justice.

7 Pierneef à La Motte
MAP F2 ■ R45 Main Rd, Franschhoek ■ 021 876 8000 ■ Closed dinner & Mon ■ RRR

The name and wines are inspired by Pierneef artworks, and the fare served here (see p37) is a modern take on traditional Cape Winelands cuisine.

8 Grande Provence Restaurant
MAP F2 ■ Main Rd, Franschhoek ■ 021 876 8600 ■ RRR

This upmarket restaurant in the estate of the same name serves an à-la-carte menu, plus a six-course wine pairing.

Elegant interior of Grande Provence

9 Café des Arts
MAP F2 ■ 7 Reservoir St West, Franschhoek ■ 021 876 2952 ■ RR

This down-to-earth bistro specializes in steaks, salads and local dishes such as bobotie, ostrich and venison.

10 The Werf Restaurant
MAP E2 ■ Pniel Rd, Groot Drakenstein ■ 021 870 4206 ■ Closed dinner Sun–Tue ■ RRR

This flagship fine-dining restaurant on the beautiful Boschendal Wine Estate (see p36) offers wine tasting, farm-to-table food and much more.

See map on p90–91

TOP 10 Beyond the Winelands

Assuming you can drag yourself away from its estimable charms, Cape Town provides a great base for exploring the rest of the Western Cape, a province notable for its consistently scenic coastline, *fynbos*-swathed mountains and ever-expanding winemaking industry. Highlights east of Cape Town include the peerless land-based whale watching in Walker Bay and the underrated De Hoop Nature Reserve – not to mention Agulhas, the most southerly tip of Africa – while the west coast up towards Lamberts Bay combines ruggedly beautiful seaside scenery with some of the world's most spectacular floral displays.

Young zebra at De Hoop

BEYOND THE WINELANDS

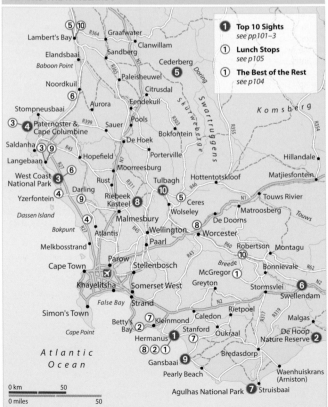

①	**Top 10 Sights** see pp101–3
①	**Lunch Stops** see p105
①	**The Best of the Rest** see p104

Lambert's Bay ⑤⑩ R364 Graafwater
Elandsbaai Sandberg Clanwilliam
Baboon Point R365 Cederberg ⑤
Noordkuil Paleisheuwel Doring
⑥ Citrusdal Swartruggens Komsberg
Stompneusbaai Aurora Eendekuil R355 R354
③④ Paternoster & R399 Sauer Pools
Cape Columbine De Hoek Bokfontein
Saldanha ③⑨ Hopefield Porterville Hillandale
Langebaan R45 Moorreesburg Hottentotskloof Matjiesfontein
West Coast ③ Rust R311 Tulbagh ⑩ N1 Touws River
National Park ④ Darling ⑨ Riebeek Ceres Matroosberg Touws
Yzerfontein Kasteel ⑧ Wolseley
Dassen Island ④ Malmesbury De Doorns
Bokpunt R27 Atlantis R45 Wellington ⑧ Worcester
Melkbosstrand Paarl R60 Robertson Montagu
  Parow R43 ⑩
Cape Town ✈ Stellenbosch *Breede* Bonnievale R62
  Khayelitsha Somerset West McGregor ① Stormsvlei ⑥
False Bay Greyton Swellendam
Simon's Town Strand N2 Rietpoel Malgas
Cape Point Betty's ⑦ Kleinmond Caledon R317 R319
  Bay ② Stanford ⑦ Oukraal De Hoop
Atlantic Hermanus ① Nature Reserve ②
Ocean ⑧②① Bredasdorp
  Gansbaai ⑨ Waenhuiskrans
0 km 50 Pearly Beach (Arniston)
0 miles 50 Agulhas National Park ⑦ Struisbaai

1 Hermanus

MAP U5 ■ **Tourist information:** **028 312 2629** ■ **www.hermanus-tourism.co.za**

Southeast of Cape Town, the quaint small town of Hermanus is perched on sheer cliffs that hem in Walker Bay. Its attractions include the montane *fynbos* of Fernkloof Nature Reserve. But above all, Hermanus is the world's best place for land-based whale viewing from June to November. The movements of southern right whales, which regularly breach in the waters below town, are tracked by a "whale crier".

2 De Hoop Nature Reserve

MAP W5 ■ **087 087 8250** ■ **Open 7am–6pm daily** ■ **Adm** ■ **www.capenature.co.za**

To the east of Agulhas, this is South Africa's largest surviving coastal *fynbos* habitat. It is a breeding ground for the endemic bontebok and Cape mountain zebra. The coastline of tall sand dunes and sheer cliffs can be explored on short walking and mountain biking trails, or along a five-day hiking trail named after the whales that breach offshore between June and November.

3 West Coast National Park

MAP S3 ■ **022 772 2144/5** ■ **Main park: open Apr–Aug: 7am–6pm daily; Sep–Mar: 7am–7pm daily** ■ **Adm** ■ **Postberg Flower Reserve: open Aug & Sep: 9am–5pm daily** ■ **Adm** ■ **www.sanparks.co.za**

Extending around the sparkling salt waters of the Langebaan Lagoon, this pristine coastline lies just an hour's drive north of Cape Town. Famous for the wild flowers in the Postberg sector, the park *(see p45)* is also worth visiting for its variety of fauna, including eland, rock hyrax and many wetland bird species. Offshore islands support breeding colonies of ten different marine bird species. The recreational zone of the lagoon is popular with watersports fans.

Wild flowers, West Coast National Park

4 Paternoster and Cape Columbine

MAP S2

The coastal village of Paternoster, located on Cape Columbine to the north of Cape Town, is renowned for its traditional white fishermen's cottages and superb crayfish. The adjacent Columbine Nature Reserve protects a lovely stretch of coast that bursts into spectacular bloom from August to October and offers excellent kayaking spots through the year.

The picturesque village of Paternoster

Prehistoric rock art on sandstone formations in the Cederberg

⑤ Cederberg
MAP U2 ■ 087 087 8250
■ www.capenature.co.za

The Cederberg Wilderness Area (provincial reserve) and the Cederberg Conservancy (private farmland) form the heart of Cederberg. The area is revered for its stunning sandstone formations, its profusion of prehistoric rock art and its rich endemic flora and fauna. It is best explored over several days, but the conservancy also offers day hikes in montane and karoo territory, with private camps providing access to rock-art sites and views.

Old Drostdy interior, Swellendam

⑥ Swellendam
MAP W5 ■ Tourist Information:
028 514 8500 ■ www.visitswellen
dam.co.za

Founded in 1745 at the Cape Colony's remote eastern frontier, this small town has an old-world atmosphere reinforced by Cape Dutch buildings such as the Old Drostdy (Magistrate's Seat), which was built in 1747 and is now a local history museum. Beyond town, lies the *renosterveld* (heath-like

land) of Bontebok National Park, established in 1931 to protect the 30 last remaining wild bontebok, whose population now numbers over 200.

⑦ Agulhas National Park
MAP V6 ■ 028 435 6078 ■ Park: open 7:30am–6pm daily ■ Lighthouse: open 9am–5pm daily ■ Adm for lighthouse ■ www.sanparks.co.za

The southernmost tip of Africa and the meeting point of the Atlantic and Indian Oceans, Agulhas, named by Portuguese navigators, means "needles", an allusion to the jagged offshore rocks that have caused around 250 shipwrecks. The park is home to South Africa's oldest lighthouse (built in 1849), and its rocky beaches have a stark charm.

⑧ Riebeek Kasteel
MAP U3 ■ Tourist information:
022 001 0096 ■ www.riebeek
valley.info

Sitting in the Swartland region north of Cape Town, Riebeek Kasteel is a favourite weekend spot for Capetonians. Best known for its olives (an

---

WHALES AND DOLPHINS

A remarkable 42 species of whales and dolphins have been recorded in South African waters. The Western Cape is the prime whale-spotting destination, thanks to the southern right whales that migrate to sheltered coves such as Walker and False bays. Bottle-nosed dolphins are regulars here too, pirouetting as they follow in a boat's wake.

annual festival honouring the olive is held here each May), Riebeek Kasteel also has a growing number of wineries producing superb reds. The historic town centre has small restaurants, a coffee roaster, two microbreweries and a chocolatier. Neighbouring Riebeek West hosts a Saturday morning produce market.

9 Gansbaai
MAP U6 ■ Tourist information: 028 384 1439 ■ www.gansbaai info.com

Boat trips from Gansbaai (Goose Bay) focus mostly on Dyer Island, which supports large numbers of marine birds, and the adjoining Geyser Island, which has a large seal colony. Subject to the season, shark cage diving takes place in the offshore shallows or in "Shark Alley", the legendary channel that divides the islands. Back on terra firma, the African Penguin & Seabird Sanctuary is a visitor-friendly rehabilitation centre for injured marine birds.

Cape fur seals at play in Gansbaai

10 Tulbagh
MAP U3 ■ Tourist information: 023 230 1375 ■ www.tulbagh tourism.co.za

The town of Tulbagh, below the Groot Winterhoek Mountains, was founded in 1700. While relatively remote from Cape Town, it makes a charming getaway. Its historical centre houses more than 30 Cape Dutch buildings, which are surrounded by imposing fynbos-draped mountains that offer good walking, horse-riding and bird-watching. The area supports over 20 wine estates.

OVERNIGHT TOUR TO HERMANUS

▶ DAY 1

Follow the N2 south-east from **Cape Town** for 45 minutes, turning right onto the R44 at **Strand** *(see p101)*. **Hermanus** is 75 km (47 miles) from Strand, so you could make it in an hour, but you'll want to stop to admire the glorious views from Clarence Drive across False Bay. **Harold Porter Botanical Garden** *(see p104)* in **Betty's Bay** is a great place to relax in a *fynbos* habitat. In Hermanus, check into a hotel and then lunch at the **Burgundy Restaurant** or grab a bite at beachfront **Dutchies** *(see p105)*. In the afternoon, follow the Cliff Path west out of town, or stroll around town keeping an eye out for whales. In calm weather, head to **Onrus Beach**. End with dinner at the Burgundy or The Marine Hermanus *(see p119)*.

▶ DAY 2

After an early breakfast, drive to **Gansbaai** for a cruise to **Dyer and Geyser Islands** to look for Cape fur seals, whales, sharks and marine birds such as African penguin, Cape gannet, Cape cormorant and black oyster-catcher. On the return trip to Gansbaai, stop at **Springfontein Eats** *(see p105)* in Stanford for lunch, then head on towards the N2 and enjoy the splendid mountain views on the **Houw Hoek** and **Sir Lowry's Pass** to **Somerset West**. If time permits, take a detour to the historic **Vergelegen Estate** *(see p93)*, located in the scenic Helderberg Mountains, and finish your day with a tasting.

See map on p100

The Best of the Rest

1 McGregor
MAP V4 ▪ 023 625 1954
▪ www.tourismmcgregor.co.za
Hidden away in the Langebergs, McGregor offers wine and olive tastings and mountain hikes.

2 Harold Porter National Botanical Garden
MAP E6 ▪ Betty's Bay ▪ 028 272 9311
▪ Open daily ▪ Adm ▪ www.sanbi.org
This garden is dedicated to *fynbos* coastal flora, and is renowned for its waterfalls and amber pools.

3 Langebaan
MAP S3 ▪ 022 772 1515
▪ www.langebaan-info.co.za
With ocean and lagoon to choose from, Langebaan is a very popular watersports destination.

4 !Khwa ttu
MAP S3 ▪ R27, Yzerfontein
▪ 022 492 2998 ▪ Tours 10am & 2pm daily ▪ Adm ▪ www.khwattu.org
!Khwa ttu explores the fascinating history and culture of South Africa's Indigenous people, the San.

5 Lambert's Bay
MAP T1 ▪ 027 432 1000
▪ www.lambertsbay.co.za
Discover Bird Island's huge colony of Cape gannets plus Heaviside's dolphins and other cetaceans via boat trips.

6 Rocherpan Nature Reserve
MAP S2 ▪ 079 203 1092
▪ Open 8am–5pm daily ▪ Adm
▪ www.capenature.co.za
The bird species in this seasonal wetland include the great white pelican and the great crested grebe.

Verdant Kogelberg Biosphere Reserve

7 Kogelberg Biosphere Reserve
MAP D5 ▪ 021 271 5138 ▪ Open 7:30am–4pm daily ▪ Adm ▪ www. capenature.co.za
A protected *fynbos* habitat that is great for hiking, biking and kayaking.

8 Karoo Desert National Botanical Garden
MAP U4 ▪ Roux Rd, Worcester ▪ 023 342 1298 ▪ Open 7am–7pm daily ▪ Adm ▪ www.sanbi.org
A largely uncultivated garden, known for its amazing displays of arid and semi-arid southern African plants.

9 Darling
MAP T3 ▪ 022 492 3361
▪ www.hellodarling.org.za
This quaint town is known for its arts and craft shops, wild flowers, tea rooms, wine and cabaret.

10 Robertson
MAP V4 ▪ 023 626 4437
▪ www.robertson-info.co.za
Robertson lies along the Breede River wine route, where the estates offer better value than those around Stellenbosch and Franschhoek.

Vineyards around Robertson

Lunch Stops

PRICE CATEGORIES

For a three-course meal for one, including half a bottle of wine, cover charge, taxes and extra charges.

R under R300 **RR** R300–400 **RRR** over R400

1 Origins at the Marine
MAP U5 ▪ Marine Dr, Hermanus ▪ 028 313 1000 ▪ **RRR**

This restaurant, in The Marine Hermanus *(see p119)*, is excellent for a seafood lunch or a three-course dinner. Enjoy a pre-meal cocktail in The Sun Lounge for views of whales breaching in the Walker Bay waters.

2 Dutchies
MAP U5 ▪ Grotto Beach, Hermanus ▪ 028 314 1392 ▪ **RR**

The cosmopolitan food served at Dutchies is enhanced by the attractive beachfront location. It's a great spot for watching whales.

3 Noisy Oyster
MAP S2 ▪ 62 St Augustine Rd, Paternoster ▪ 022 752 2196 ▪ Closed Mon & Tue, dinner Sun ▪ **RR**

As the name suggests, seafood is the main focus of the menu here. Diners rave about West Coast oysters and mussels and the seafood *laksa*, a Malaysian-style spicy soup.

4 Hilda's Kitchen
MAP T3 ▪ R27, Darling ▪ 022 492 2825 ▪ Closed Mon & Tue, dinner Wed–Sun ▪ **RR**

Based within the Groote Post winery, Hilda's specializes in tasty country cooking. The menu changes daily, but a good range of meat, fish and pasta dishes can usually be expected.

5 Tolhuis Bistro
MAP U3 ▪ R43, Mitchell's Pass, Ceres ▪ 023 312 1211 ▪ Closed Mon, dinner Tue–Sun ▪ **R**

Named after a former toll house (now a national monument) at Mitchell's Pass, this place serves great steaks and light lunches.

6 Geelbek Restaurant
MAP S3 ▪ West Coast National Park ▪ 084 406 7434 ▪ Closed dinner ▪ **RR**

Set in a Cape Dutch house, Geelbek specializes in South African fare.

7 Springfontein Eats
MAP U5 ▪ 8 Wortelgat Rd, Stanford ▪ 028 341 0571 ▪ Closed lunch Mon–Wed, dinner Sun–Tue ▪ **RRR**

Set on a working wine farm, this restaurant serves a three- to six-course tasting menu created with fresh ingredients from the farm's vegetable garden. Extensive wine list.

Characterful, elegant Burgundy

8 Burgundy Restaurant
MAP U5 ▪ Marine Dr, Hermanus ▪ 028 312 2800 ▪ **RR**

This sea view restaurant has an excellent Mediterranean-style menu. Now a heritage site, it's set in one of the oldest buildings in Hermanus.

9 Die Strandloper
MAP S3 ▪ Langebaan Lagoon ▪ 022 772 2490 ▪ Closed Mon–Fri ▪ No credit cards, cash or EFT only ▪ **RRR**

This place serves a tasty barbecued fish buffet. As this is weather dependent, booking is essential.

10 Muisbosskerm Restaurant
MAP S1 ▪ R365, 4 km (2 miles) south of Lambert's Bay ▪ 027 432 1017 ▪ **RR**

Linger over the buffet of Cape seafood dishes at this open-air restaurant on the beachfront.

See map on p100

Streetsmart

Brightly painted traditional houses
in the Bo-Kaap district of Cape Town

Getting Around

Arriving by Air

The main gateway for international flights to South Africa is **OR Tambo International Airport** in Johannesburg. It is connected to Cape Town by numerous domestic flights. A few carriers also fly directly to Cape Town from Europe or the Middle East, including **British Airways**, **Emirates**, **Lufthansa** and **KLM**.

Cape Town International Airport flanks the N2 highway 20 km (12 miles) east of the city centre. Regular flights connect Cape Town to Durban and Johannesburg, with less frequent services to Gqeberha (formerly Port Elizabeth), Bloemfontein and other South African cities. Fares with **South African Airways** tend to be pricier so seek out the budget operators **Mango**, **Kulula** and **Safair**.

The cheapest way to get from the airport to the city is on the MyCiTi bus, which leaves every 30 minutes and takes 25–30 minutes to get to the city centre. Registered taxi operators and shuttle services have stands in the airport, and most hotels can arrange transfers on request.

Arriving by Sea

Cape Town is a port of call for cruise ships heading between the Indian Ocean Islands and Europe. Cape Town Cruise Terminal at the **Port of Cape Town** is a 10-minute drive from the city centre and within walking distance of the V&A Waterfront.

Intercity Trains

Shosholoza Meyl is the main rail operator, with routes to Johannesburg and East London, but passenger services are infrequent. There are also two luxurious and expensive options – the **Blue Train**, which travels between Cape Town and Pretoria, and **Rovos Rail**, which travels to Pretoria and on to Victoria Falls.

Suburban Trains

The most useful train route is **Metrorail**'s Southern Line, which runs to Simon's Town and includes a very scenic stretch from Kalk Bay onwards. There's also a regular service to Stellenbosch. Buy a ticket before boarding and keep an eye on the stations you pass – there are no route maps or announcements on board. Trains are fine during the day, but avoid empty carriages and travelling after dark.

Local Buses

MyCiTi is Cape Town's main bus operator. Safety and hygiene measures, timetables, ticket information, maps and more can be obtained from the MyCiti website. To travel on the buses, you need to purchase a prepaid card for R35. This can then be topped up at certain stores, some ATMs and at major MyCiTi bus terminals. If you want to use the airport bus but won't be taking public transport afterwards, there is a single trip card available

from the airport to the city centre and/or the V&A Waterfront for R80.

Older **Golden Arrow** buses also operate around town and the suburbs, but they're not as comprehensive or user-friendly. Cash is accepted on board.

Minibus Taxis

Shared combi taxis are ubiquitous and the main form of public transport for locals. They can be hailed and are cheap, but you'll often wait a while for the seats to fill up. Still, they offer a snapshot of local life and are fine for short trips. Pay the driver's assistant once you have boarded – fares start at R8 for a short journey.

Long-Distance Bus Travel

Safe, comfortable and affordable coach services cover most main routes in South Africa. **Intercape** buses connect Cape Town to major cities and popular tourist towns. **Adderley Street Bus Station** is the main terminal, and is located next to the train station.

Taxis

Taxis in the city are good value at around R10/km. It's best to book ahead with a reputable operator such as **Excite**, **Rikki's** or **Intercab**, as they cannot usually be hailed on the street. The private taxi app **Uber** operates in Cape Town, the airport and some locations in the Winelands.

Car Rental

Rates start at around R90–150 per day and usually include 200 km (124 miles) free usage, though some offer unlimited mileage. International operators such as **Avis** and **Hertz** are costlier than local companies such as **Around About Cars** and **Tempest**, though the best deals are usually found through consolidators such as **Argus Car Hire**.

Parking

Paid street parking is ample in the city at reasonable rates. Outside the city centre, you won't find a meter but you will often find a car guard. These self-employed people will keep an eye on your car in return for small change – R5 during the day and R10 at night.

Rules of the Road

South Africa drives on the left side of the road. Speed limits are usually 120 kmph (75 mph) on major highways, and speed cameras are common. Look out for rapid drops in the speed limit. If you're stopped by police, never pay a fine at the side of the road – always insist on a ticket and pay the fine at a post office later on.

Cycle Hire

Cape Town is a bike-friendly city with a growing network of dedicated cycle lanes. **Bicycle Cape Town** has information on routes, laws and bike rental. **Up Cycles** rents out bicycles at various locations in and around the city centre.

Walking

Most major attractions in central Cape Town are within walking distance of each other, and there are numerous walking tours available. Take advice from trusted locals about where not to go after dark.

DIRECTORY

Practical Information

Passports and Visas

For entry requirements, including visas, consult your nearest South African embassy or check with the country's **Department of Home Affairs (DHA)**. Citizens of the UK, United States, Canada, Australia, New Zealand and most European Union countries can stay in South Africa visa-free for up to 90 days on production of a valid passport at the point of entry. Citizens of most other countries will need to buy a visa in advance.

Government Advice

Now more than ever, it is important to consult both your and the South African government's advice before travelling. The **UK Foreign and Commonwealth Office**, the **US State Department**, the **Australian Department of Foreign Affairs and Trade** and the South African Department of Home Affairs offer the latest information on security, health and local regulations.

Customs Information

You can find information on the laws relating to goods and currency taken in or out of South Africa on the **South African Tourist Board** website. No duty is charged on items that are imported temporarily for personal use, and duty-free restrictions are standard. Non-residents can claim a VAT refund on leaving the country if the items they purchased can be inspected, so ask for a tax invoice when you buy expensive items.

Insurance

We recommend that you take out a comprehensive insurance policy covering theft, loss of belongings, medical care, cancellations and delays, and read the small print carefully. There is no public health service, which means that any medical bills of uninsured travellers will have to be paid by them at the time of treatment.

Health

State and provincial hospitals offer adequate facilities, but tend to be under-funded and under-staffed; the standard of private healthcare is high. South Africa does not have reciprocal health-care agreements with other countries, so pay-ment of medical expenses is the responsibility of the patient. It is therefore important to arrange comprehensive medical insurance before travelling.

The Cape Town area has several excellent private hospitals including branches of **Mediclinic** and **Netcare**. **Groote Schuur** is a superb public hospital with an emer-gency department.

Vaccinations advised for most tropical countries aren't really applicable to the Cape Town area, although you should get polio or tetanus boosters, if these have expired.

Anyone travelling to Cape Town via a yellow fever area might be asked to show a vaccination certificate at immigration. For information regarding COVID-19 vaccination requirements, consult government advice.

Most pharmacies keep standard business hours, but there are late-night and even 24-hour ones. The **Lite-Kem Pharmacy** is open until 8pm daily.

Tap water is safe to drink in South Africa unless stated otherwise.

Smoking, Alcohol and Drugs

Smoking is illegal and socially unacceptable in buses, trains, taxis, restaurants and most public buildings.

Alcohol is served in practically all hotels and licensed restaurants, as well as in bars. The consumption of alcohol on beaches is illegal, and drink driving legislation is strictly enforced.

The personal con-sumption of cannabis by adults in private was decriminalized in 2018, but laws prohibiting buying and selling it, or consuming it in public, remain in place. Travellers caught using illegal drugs may be arrested and face a heavy fine or jail time.

ID

It is not required to carry ID on one's person. Drivers must be in possession of their driving license when behind the wheel.

Personal Security

Although South Africa has a reputation when it comes to crime, it's fairly rare for a tourist to encounter anything other than the usual petty crime associated with larger cities. Take sensible precautions when walking around – don't flash your cash or valuables, lock away jewellery, passports and other valuables, avoid deserted parts of town and be vigilant after dark. Avoid the city's townships at night unless you're on an organized tour, and be sure that your ride home is in a registered taxi.

There have been some attacks on hikers walking the many footpaths of Table Mountain. Never hike alone and always tell someone which route you'll be taking.

Carjackings are incredibly rare in Cape Town but do be vigilant when waiting at red lights.

Two scams have been associated with ATMs.

One involves a "helpful" local making off with your card; the other entails causing your card to get stuck mid-transaction. You are most vulnerable outside of banking hours and in remote locations.

If you are mugged, do not challenge the thief – hand over your belongings immediately and call the police afterwards.

In an emergency, there are two central phone numbers for **Ambulance/ Fire**, and for **Police**. There is also a separate **emergency number from a mobile (cell) phone**.

Apartheid legislation was repealed in 1991 and a new constitution that afforded equal rights to all racial groups has been in effect since 1996, although the legacy of segregation can still be felt in some areas. The rights of gay people are also enshrined in the constitution and gay marriage has been legal since 2006. But while Cape Town is certainly the LGBTQ+ capital of Africa, smaller towns and rural areas retain more conservative attitudes. If you do feel unsafe, the **Safe Space Alliance** pinpoints your nearest place of refuge.

Travellers with Specific Requirements

Most hotels, malls and tourist sights in South Africa have wheelchair access. Some public transport is accessible to wheelchairs, including MyCiTi buses and the City Sightseeing Bus. Larger taxis with ramps can be booked in advance.

If you rent a car, ask for a parking disc that allows for concessions. Some car-hire companies have vehicles with hand controls for drivers with disabilities.

Tour operators such as **Flamingo Tours**, **Epic Enabled** and **Endeavour Safaris** specialize in itineraries for travellers with specific requirements.

DIRECTORY

PASSPORTS AND VISAS

Department of Home Affairs (DHA)
w dha.gov.za

GOVERNMENT ADVICE

Australian Department of Foreign Affairs and Trade
w smartraveller.gov.au

UK Foreign and Commonwealth Office
w gov.uk/foreign-travel-advice

US Department of State
w travel.state.gov

CUSTOMS INFORMATION

South African Tourist Board
w southafrica.net

HEALTH

Groote Schuur
Main Rd, Observatory
w gsh.co.za

Lite-Kem Pharmacy
24 Darling St
w litekem.co.za

Mediclinic
w mediclinic.co.za

Netcare
w netcare.co.za

PERSONAL SECURITY

Ambulance/Fire
☏ 10177

Police
☏ 10111

Emergency number from a mobile (cell) phone
☏ 112

Safe Space Alliance
w safespacealliance.com

Travellers with specific requirements

Endeavour Safaris
w endeavour-safaris.com

Epic Enabled
w epic-enabled.com

Flamingo Tours
w flamingotours.co.za

Time Zone

South Africa uses South Africa Standard Time, which is always 2 hours ahead of Greenwich Mean Time, and 6 hours ahead of the US Eastern Standard Summer Time.

Money

South Africa's currency is the rand, made up of 100 cents. It is locally denoted by the letter R, and internationally by ZAR. Bank notes are in denominations of R10, R20, R50, R100 and R200. Coins are 10c, 20c, 50c, R1, R2, R5.

Most banks are open 9am–3:30pm Monday–Friday. City banks are open 8:30–11:30am on Saturday.

ATMs are widespread, including at all airports. You can use them to draw local currency with any major international credit or debit card and they generally offer the best rate of exchange. Banks and bureaux de change are also plentiful. Most businesses accept major credit cards, but keep your card in sight when making a payment, especially in restaurants, to reduce the risk of it being "cloned". Informal traders do not usually accept credit cards, and it is advisable to carry some cash with you in rural areas just in case.

Electrical Appliances

The South African plug has three round pins, though most hotel and guesthouse rooms also have sockets (or adaptors) for the twin-pronged plugs used in continental Europe. For appliances with any other plug, it's advisable to bring adaptors. The electricity supply is 220-230v/50Hz.

Mobile Phones and Wi-Fi

Cape Town has a 021 prefix, and the international code for South Africa is +27. Calls out of South Africa are prefixed by 00. Mobile (cell) phone numbers start with 06, 07 or 08. If you are set up for international roaming, you can use your GSM phone in South Africa. A cheaper alternative is to buy a local SIM card, which comes with pre-paid talk time and data. You need to "RICA" (register) your SIM before using it. To do this, you'll need a passport and proof of your address in South Africa in the form of a reservation confirmation, which can be supplied by your hotel or other accommodation.

Most hotels also offer internet facilities, but make sure it's free. Many bars, restaurants, cafés, guesthouses and hostels also offer free Wi-Fi. At airports, you'll need to sign up to access the Wi-Fi.

Postal Services

International post through the **South African Post Office** tends to be slow – airmail to Europe takes at least two weeks and to North America even longer – and it is also increasingly unreliable. A faster service is offered by a private chain called **PostNet**, found in most large malls. Use an international courier for items of any value.

Weather

The warm summer months of November to February are peak tourist season. Winter has periods of beautiful, mild weather interspersed with days of cold, rain and wind. Late August–October is the best time to visit; it's not too crowded, the weather is mild and the spring wild flowers are on display.

Opening Hours

Post offices and government offices are open 8:30am to 4:30pm Monday to Friday. Post offices are also open 8:30 to 11:30am on Saturdays. Timings for sights do vary, so always check ahead.

COVID-19 Increased rates of infection may result in temporary opening hours and/or closures. Always check ahead before visiting museums, attractions and hospitality venues.

Visitor Information

The main **Cape Town Tourism** office is in the city centre and it offers general information on the city and Western Cape province. There are also offices at popular tourist spots such as Table Mountain and the V&A Waterfront, and at the airport. **Franschhoek**, **Stellenbosch** and the **Winelands** all have their own tourism websites. Cape Town also has a host of blogs and lifestyle apps and magazines.

Zomato is a nationwide restaurant-rating website and app. **EatOut** is great for anything food-related. **Mother City Living** focuses on markets and environmentally friendly happenings. **Cape Town Magazine** and **What's on in Cape Town** are also great for finding out about local events.

If you are planning to visit multiple attractions in the city, it may be worth investing in a Cape Town City Pass from Cape Town Tourism. There are three different types of pass available, offering savings on admission to many of the city's top sights.

Local Customs

South Africa is a relatively cosmopolitan country, and visitors are unlikely to find themselves in any situations where they are culturally out of their depth. The dress code here is casual, except for at a few top restaurants and formal events. On the beach, it is illegal for women to swim or sunbathe topless.

Visitors should observe appropriate religious customs when visiting mosques, churches, temples and other places of worship.

Sustainable Travel

Cape Town has suffered from a series of severe droughts and water scarcity is an ongoing concern. Many eco friendly accommodation providers collect and recycle water (among other conservation strategies), but you can also play a part in reducing water consumption by taking quick showers and re-using towels.

Before booking a township tour, check that it will be conducted responsibly by asking the operator whether your guide will be from the township and whether a portion of the fee will be returned to the community.

Language

South Africa has 12 official languages: Afrikaans, English, IsiNdebele, IsiXhosa, IsiZulu, North Sotho, SeTswana, SiSwati, South African Sign Language, South Sotho, TshiVenda and XiTsonga. English is very widely spoken, especially in the tourist industry.

Taxes and Refunds

A 15 per cent VAT is levied on all purchases and services other than a select list of essential grocery items such as bread and milk. It is permitted for visitors to reclaim VAT on any goods bought to export home. This can be done at the VAT reclaim desk at any international airport or border post, provided you can produce the original receipts.

Accommodation

Accommodation ranges from backpacker dorms to family-friendly budget hotels and five-star resorts. Self-catering accommodation is easy to find. Local booking sites include **WhereToStay** and **SafariNow**. **Airbnb** is also very popular in Cape Town. **Booking.com** has some good deals.

Prices vary hugely, from hostel en-suite doubles at around R600 a night to luxury suites that cost over R10,000. At peak times (Christmas and Easter) prices can skyrocket, and rooms need to be booked up months in advance.

Places to Stay

PRICE CATEGORIES

For a standard, double room per night (with breakfast if included), taxes and extra charges.

R under R1500   RR R1500–2500   RRR over R2500

Luxury Hotels

Westin Cape Town
MAP Q3 ■ 1 Lower Long St ■ 021 412 9999 ■ www.westincapetown.com ■ RR
Geared towards business travellers, this hotel towers over the Cape Town International Convention Centre (CTICC). The rooms are well-appointed and have all the standard five-star facilities.

Belmond Mount Nelson Hotel
MAP P6 ■ 76 Orange St, Gardens ■ 021 483 1000 ■ www.belmond.com ■ RRR
With its iconic Victorian exteriors, elegant rooms, a fine-dining restaurant and grand views, the "Nellie" is undoubtedly the city's most prestigious hotel. The afternoon teas served with obsequious gravity on the patio are highly recommended.

Camps Bay Retreat
MAP G1 ■ 7 Chilworth Rd, Camps Bay ■ 021 437 8300 ■ www.campsbayretreat.com ■ RRR
Tucked away in a private nature reserve near the ocean, this historic property has rooms in the main house or in a separate building reached by a rope bridge across a ravine. Children are welcome, but the spa and rambling gardens also make it a peaceful spot for honeymooners.

Cape Grace
MAP Q2 ■ West Quay Rd, V&A Waterfront ■ 021 410 7100 ■ www.capegrace.com ■ RRR
The aptly named Cape Grace hotel offers stylish accommodation, a mind-boggling array of services, tasty Cape fusion cuisine and informal but attentive staff. Some rooms have private balconies.

Cape Heritage Hotel
MAP P4 ■ 90 Bree St ■ 021 424 4646 ■ www.capeheritage.co.za ■ RRR
This historic hotel has 17 individually decorated rooms with antique features such as 19th-century wood floors and high-beamed ceilings. South Africa's oldest grapevine is located in the courtyard.

The Cape Milner
MAP N5 ■ 2a Milner Rd, Tamboerskloof ■ 021 426 1101 ■ www.capemilner.com ■ RRR
A chic city hotel with 57 rooms decorated with flair in a refreshingly minimalist style. Services include a cocktail and tapas lounge, swimming pool and gym.

One&Only Cape Town
MAP P2 ■ Dock Rd, V&A Waterfront ■ 021 431 5800 ■ www.oneandonlyresorts.com ■ RRR
An urban resort with contemporary African flair, set in the heart of the trendy V&A Waterfront. It has 131 rooms and suites, 40 of them on an island in the marina.

The Twelve Apostles Hotel & Spa
MAP G2 ■ Victoria Rd, Camps Bay ■ 021 437 9000 ■ www.12apostleshotel.com ■ RRR
Located on the edge of the Atlantic Ocean and at the foot of the Twelve Apostles formation, this five-star boutique hotel has 70 exceptional rooms, superb service, a private cinema and an excellent spa. It also offers guided walks and picnics in the surrounding *fynbos*.

Victoria & Alfred Hotel
MAP P2 ■ Pierhead, V&A Waterfront ■ 021 419 6677 ■ www.newmarkhotels.com ■ RRR
Located in a converted Victorian warehouse, this hotel rises from the heart of the V&A Waterfront, ensuring that all the airy rooms have good views. Loft suites come with a heavier price tag than standard rooms.

Waterfront Village
MAP Q2 ■ 4 West Quay Rd, V&A Waterfront ■ 021 421 5040 ■ www.waterfrontvillage.com ■ RRR
A five-star apartment-and-suite complex that offers luxury self-catering accommodation, sleeping from two to six people. The many amenities, including five swimming pools, make it suitable for couples and families.

Mid-Range Hotels

Cape Standard
MAP M2 ■ 3 Romney Rd, Green Point ■ 021 430 3060 ■ www.cape standard.co.za ■ RR
A boutique guesthouse, Cape Standard combines sleek modern European minimalism with subtle African touches to create a light, spacious feel. It's within striking distance of the V&A Waterfront.

Derwent House
MAP N6 ■ 14 Derwent Rd, Tamboerskloof ■ 021 422 2763 ■ www.derwent house.co.za ■ RR
This boutique hotel, set in the heart of the City Bowl, has rooms with private terraces and great views. The stylish decor is complemented by excellent facilities, including a large deck, solar-heated pool and hot tub.

Peninsula All-Suite Hotel
MAP J4 ■ 313 Beach Rd, Sea Point ■ 021 430 7777 ■ www.peninsula.co.za ■ RR
This seafront Art Deco high-rise hotel offers spectacular views and has self-catering apartments. Facilities include a pool and a complimentary shuttle to various sites. The surrounding area has a range of shops. The hotel is popular with families and small groups.

The Three Boutique Hotel
MAP P7 ■ 3 Flower St, Oranjezicht ■ 021 424 1530 ■ www.thethree.co.za ■ RR
Historic and modern combine in this boutique hotel housed in a lovely colonnade-fronted building dating back to 1740. Guests can relax in the wraparound verandah, on the pool terrace or on the rooftop sundeck that has stunning views of Table Mountain.

Villa Zest
MAP P2 ■ 2 Braemar Rd, Green Point ■ 021 433 1246 ■ www.villazest.co.za ■ RR
With suites given names such as Barbarella and Xanadu, you can expect something a little different here. The interior design is striking – from the eclectic art in the communal areas to the individually designed 1970s-inspired rooms. Excellent service and fabulous breakfasts complete the package.

Four Rosmead
MAP N7 ■ 4 Rosmead Ave, Oranjezicht ■ 021 480 3810 ■ www.four rosmead.com ■ RRR
Built in 1903, this boutique guesthouse is set in a classified monument that has been stylishly remodelled. The interiors are subtle but feature distinctive local South African art. Facilities here include a pamper room and a patio overlooking a pool.

Winchester Mansions
MAP L2 ■ 221 Beach Rd, Sea Point ■ 021 434 2351 ■ www.winchester.co.za ■ RRR
A 1920s building set around a bougainvillea-clad courtyard and right on the promenade at Sea Point. Rooms on the lower floor have a floral Edwardian feel, while those on the upper floors are spacious and modern.

Budget Hotels

Daddy Long Legs
MAP P4 ■ 134 Long St ■ 021 422 3074 ■ www.daddylonglegs.co.za ■ R
Situated at the heart of Long Street, this bold boutique hotel has 13 rooms, each of which has been uniquely decorated by different artists.

The New Tulbagh Hotel
MAP Q4 ■ 9 Ryk Tulbagh Square ■ 021 418 5161 ■ www.newtulbaghhotel.com ■ R
The rooms at this centrally located hotel are simple and spacious. Rates include a buffet-style breakfast. It's close to the train and bus stations and also only a short stroll from the V&A Waterfront.

President Hotel
MAP J5 ■ 4 Alexander Rd, Bantry Bay ■ 021 434 8111 ■ www.president hotel.co.za ■ RR
Expect four-star amenities at budget-friendly prices at this handsome high rise with a large swimming pool.

Southern Suburbs & Peninsula Hotels

The Andros Deluxe Boutique Hotel
MAP H2 ■ Cnr Newlands & Phyllis Rds, Claremont ■ 021 797 9777 ■ www.andros.co.za ■ RR
This hotel is set in a 1908 Cape Dutch homestead. All 15 rooms have verandas and are sumptuously furnished with antiques. There is also a suite with a private pool. Facilities include a gym, beauty salon and a candlelit country restaurant.

Quayside Hotel
MAP H4 ■ Jubilee Sq, St George's St, Simon's Town ■ 021 786 3838 ■ www.aha.co.za/quayside ■ RR
Located above the Quayside Centre (see p88), this four-star hotel has wonderful views. The 26 rooms here are very spacious, and it's well worth paying the slight premium for a sea-facing one with a balcony.

The Cellars-Hohenort
MAP H2 ■ 93 Brommersvlei Rd, Constantia ■ 021 794 2137 ■ www.collectionmcgrath.com ■ RRR
An elegant five-star hotel, Cellars-Hohenort is set in grounds bordering Kirstenbosch National Botanical Garden. It has a very classy set-up, with a strong period feel and two excellent restaurants, one of which, Greenhouse (see p81), offers fresh, seasonal menus and wine-pairing.

Glen Avon Lodge
MAP H2 ■ 1 Strawberry Ln, Constantia ■ 021 794 1418 ■ www.glenavon.co.za ■ RRR
Situated in the heart of the Constantia winelands, this well-established, five-star lodge is notable for the four-course dinner served in a 200-year-old Cape Dutch homestead.

The Last Word Constantia
MAP H2 ■ Spaanschemat River Rd, Constantia ■ 021 794 7657 ■ www.thelastword.co.za ■ RRR
This boutique hotel has four superior doubles and five suites. The interior combines contemporary decor with a scattering of modern African art. The hotel operates primarily as a B&B, but staff can prepare meals on request, or you can explore the nearby dining options.

Steenberg Hotel
MAP H3 ■ Steenberg Estate, Tokai ■ 021 713 2222 ■ www.steenbergfarm.com ■ RRR
This intimate five-star hotel on the Steenberg Estate has fine thatched-and-gabled Cape Dutch architecture. There are two excellent restaurants, Catharina's and Bistro Sixteen82 (see p81). Guests can also access the Steenberg Golf Course.

Tintswalo at Boulders Boutique Villa
MAP H4 ■ 7 Gay Rd, Simons Town ■ 021 612 0113, ■ www.tintswalo.com ■ RRR
Comprising nine luxurious suites, this beautiful villa offers excellent service and food in a prime location that overlooks the penguin colony at Boulders.

Tintswalo Atlantic
MAP G3 ■ Chapman's Peak Drive, Hout Bay ■ 021 201 0025 ■ www.tintswalo.com ■ RRR
Hanging over the Atlantic Ocean on Chapman's Peak Drive, this five-star resort boasts one of the best locations of any hotel in Cape Town. The utterly gorgeous suites combine classic decor with modern touches, and reflect the beauty of their natural surroundings. Facilities include a fabulous pool on a wooden deck just metres from the ocean.

Vineyard Hotel
MAP H2 ■ 60 Colinton Rd, Newlands ■ 021 657 4500 ■ www.vineyard.co.za ■ RRR
The Vineyard is centred around a 1799 country manor, set in a lush riverside garden estate, which was built for the Scottish traveller and society hostess Lady Anne Barnard. This luxurious hotel offers a variety of rooms, a quartet of restaurants – including a sushi bar – and two heated swimming pools.

Winelands Town Hotels

Batavia Boutique Hotel
MAP D2 ■ 12 Louw St, Stellenbosch ■ 021 887 2914 ■ www.batavia-stellenbosch.co.za ■ RR
Experience the grandeur of a classical 19th-century guesthouse, but with all modern conveniences. The Batavia's nine luxurious suites are all individually designed with carefully selected antique and contemporary pieces.

Akademie Street Boutique Hotel
MAP F2 ■ 5 Akademie St, Franschhoek ■ 082 517 0405 ■ www.aka.co.za ■ RRR
In a quiet side-street just a short walk from the town centre, Akademie is made up of luxurious suites in various buildings scattered around the garden. Three rooms have their own private pools, while the other three share a larger pool. An incredibly peaceful place to stay.

Coopmanhuijs Boutique Hotel

MAP D2 ■ 33 Church St, Stellenbosch ■ 021 883 8207 ■ www.coopman huijs.co.za ■ RRR

Set within an 18th-century heritage building, the 16 compact rooms at this boutique hotel have plenty of character. Some rooms have good-sized balconies, and there is a charming streetside terrace, where you can sip a glass of local wine while watching the world go by. There is also a pool and Helena's Restaurant (see p98).

Grande Roche Hotel

MAP E1 ■ Plantasie St, Paarl ■ 021 863 5100 ■ www.granderoche.com ■ RRR

One of the top hotels in the Winelands, set at the foot of magnificent Paarl Rock, Grande Roche is built around a lovely Cape Dutch manor, now listed as a national monument. Its 34 suites have wonderful views.

Mont Rochelle

MAP F2 ■ Dassenberg Rd, Franschhoek ■ 021 876 2770 ■ www.virgin limitededition.com/en/ mont-rochelle ■ RRR

This five-star hotel on the Mont Rochelle Wine Estate offers fabulous views over Franschhoek. Built in the classic Cape Dutch style, it has 26 elegant rooms and suites, two fine restaurants, a spa and a heated outdoor pool.

Oude Werf Hotel

MAP D2 ■ 30 Church St, Stellenbosch ■ 021 887 4608 ■ www.oudewerf. co.za ■ RRR

Established in 1802 on the foundations of a fire-damaged church, this institution is South Africa's oldest country inn. It has an atmospheric ambience and a handy location on historic Church Street. It offers 58 rooms and a fine Cape restaurant.

Winelands Rural Hotels

Cascade Country Manor

MAP E1 ■ Waterval Rd, Nederburg, Paarl ■ 021 868 0227 ■ www.cascade manor.co.za ■ RR

Perched at the end of a gravel road some 10 km (6 miles) outside of Paarl, Cascade Country Manor is named for the small waterfall found at the end of a path cutting through the olive grove. Rooms edge the manicured lawns, with terraces overlooking the pool area.

The Devon Valley Hotel

MAP D2 ■ Devon Valley Rd, near Stellenbosch ■ 021 865 2012 ■ www.devon valleyhotel.com ■ RR

Set on the Sylvanvale Estate, this popular, four-star country retreat offers lovely views and retains an elegant Edwardian feel. Guests can stroll through the surrounding vineyards or dine in the award-winning Flavours Restaurant.

Kleine Zalze Lodge

MAP D3 ■ R44, Stellenbosch ■ 021 880 0740 ■ www.kleine zalze.co.za ■ RR

This lodge offers four-star accommodation (with the option for self-catering) close to Stellenbosch. Set among oak trees with mountain and golf-course views, the hotel has the Kleine Zalze restaurant (see p98).

Spier Hotel

MAP D3 ■ Spier Wine Farm, R310, Stellenbosch ■ 021 809 1100 ■ www. spier.co.za ■ RR

This four-star hotel overlooks the Eerste River on Spier Farm, a short drive from Stellenbosch. The 153 contemporary rooms are arranged around six courtyards. It also has a pool.

WedgeView Country House & Spa

MAP D3 ■ Bonniemile Rd, Stellenbosch ■ 021 881 3525 ■ www.wedge view.co.za ■ RR

Indulge in five-star luxury at this private country residence with 18 individually decorated rooms, heated pools and a spa. There are magnificent views of the surrounding vineyards.

Asara Wine Estate & Hotel

MAP D3 ■ Polkadraai Rd, Stellenbosch ■ 021 888 8000 ■ www.asara.co.za ■ RRR

With 40 rooms, this is one of the larger hotels in the Winelands and offers fine views and wine tasting. There's a pool, three restaurants, spa treatments and a walking trail through the vineyards.

Boschendal Farm

MAP F2 ■ Helshoogte Rd, Franschhoek ■ 021 870 4200 ■ www. boschendal.com ■ RRR

Secluded and spacious self-catering cottages with country-style décor set in the grounds of the Cape's second-oldest wine estate.

Eikendal Lodge
MAP D3 ■ R44 south of Stellenbosch ■ 021 855 3617 ■ www.eiken dallodge.co.za ■ RRR
This vine-draped lodge is set among the Eikendal Estate vineyards. There is an excellent Italian restaurant, and facilities include a fly-fishing clinic as well as plenty of other outdoor activities.

Lanzerac
MAP E3 ■ 1 Lanzerac Rd, Stellenbosch ■ 021 887 1132 ■ www.lanzerac. co.za ■ RRR
This prestigious hotel is centred on a handsome 300-year-old Cape Dutch estate. Equipped with five-star facilities including a spa, the whole set-up positively exudes luxury.

La Petite Ferme
MAP F2 ■ Franschhoek Pass Rd, Franschhoek ■ 021 876 3016 ■ www. lapetiteferme.co.za ■ RRR
The view over the entire Franschhoek wine valley from these suites and self-catering cottages is mesmerizing. There's a well-regarded restaurant (see p99) and intimate winery, so you can eat and drink in style.

Le Quartier Français
MAP F2 ■ Wilhelmina & Berg Sts, Franschhoek ■ 021 876 2151 ■ www. leeucollection.com/SA/ le-quartier-francais ■ RRR
This legendary five-star hotel offers 21 rooms and suites around the rose-filled courtyard and the swimming pool; each has lounges and artworks by local artists. It is also highly acclaimed for its restaurant, La Petite Colombe (see p58).

The Light House
MAP E1 ■ 2 Lille St, Courtrai, Paarl ■ 021 863 4600 ■ www.thelight house.co.za ■ RRR
Expect tip-top service at this boutique guesthouse, set amid vineyards. The five large suites boast sumptuous decor and overlook the expansive gardens and pool.

Hotels Beyond the Winelands

Farr Out Guesthouse
MAP S2 ■ 17 Seemeeus-ingel, Paternoster ■ 022 752 2222 ■ www.farrout. co.za ■ R
This establishment, located on the outskirts of Paternoster, offers four rooms and a rustic but plush wigwam tent in the fynbos field. Two of the rooms have balconies with sea views. It is the perfect place to enjoy the wonderful natural sights of Cape Columbine.

The Great White House
MAP U6 ■ Geelbek Rd, Kleinbaai, Gansbaai ■ 028 384 3273 ■ www. thegreatwhitehouse. co.za ■ R
The main hub for marine trips to Dyer Island and other activities, this lodge offers comfortable cottages and à la carte dining, a few paces from the jetty.

Old Mac Daddy Luxury Trailer Park
MAP F4 ■ Valley Rd, Elgin ■ 021 884 0241 ■ www. oldmacdaddy.co.za ■ R
Long, sleek Airstream trailers were imported from the US to create this part-caravan-park/ part-designer-farm

resort. Each of the iconic vehicles in the park has been decorated by an artist in über-modern, often outrageous themes. This charmingly eccentric place is about an hour's drive east of Cape Town.

Abalone Guest Lodge
MAP U5 ■ 306 Main Rd, Hermanus ■ 044 533 1345 ■ www.abalone lodge.co.za ■ RR
Situated on Sievers Point, this pleasantly decorated guesthouse is ideal for cliff walks, superb land-based whale watching and exploring the small town centre of Hermanus.

Agulhas Country Lodge
MAP V6 ■ Main Rd, L'Agulhas ■ 028 435 7650 ■ www.agulhas countrylodge.com ■ RR
Set on a hill overlooking the southernmost point in Africa, this family-run guesthouse offers just eight rooms, all with great views. The lodge's fine-dining res-taurant serves some of the best seafood on the south coast.

Misty Waves Boutique Hotel
MAP U5 ■ 21 Marine Dr, Hermanus ■ 028 313 8460 ■ www.hermanus mistybeach.co.za ■ RR
A curvaceous building on the cliffs, with a lounge, pool, private Jacuzzi and a great sea-food restaurant with stunning views across the bay. It's also an excellent place for whale watching.

Cliff Lodge
MAP U6 ■ 6 Cliff St,
De Kelders, Gansbaai
■ 028 384 0983 ■ www.
clifflodge.co.za ■ RRR
Located on a magnificent
clifftop outside Gansbaai,
this place offers spectacular views of Walker Bay,
and features four spacious
rooms, a suite and a self-
catering cottage. There's
also a shared conservatory
and deck with ocean
views, and a plunge pool.

The Marine Hermanus
MAP U5 ■ Marine Dr,
Hermanus ■ 028 313
1000 ■ www.themarine
hotel.co.za ■ RRR
The very best address in
Hermanus offers accom-
modation in rooms and
suites. The patio is a
vantage point for whale
watching, and facilities
include a spa, tidal pool
and two great restaurants.

Robertson Small Hotel
MAP V4 ■ 58 Van
Reenen St, Robertson
■ 023 626 7200 ■ www.
therobertsonsmallhotel.
com ■ RRR
This grand Victorian
home offers the smartest
accommodation in town
and has a fine in-house
restaurant. The sleepy
valley of wine and olives
is a popular weekend
escape from Cape Town.

Backpacker Hostels

Ashanti Hostel
MAP P6 ■ 11 Hof St,
Gardens ■ 021 423 8721
■ Breakfast excl ■ www.
ashanti.co.za ■ R
Combining upmarket
decor with a relaxed party
atmosphere, this place

serves meals and drinks
in the bar. The deck has
views of Table Mountain.

The Backpack
MAP N5 ■ 74 New
Church St, Tamboerskloof
■ 021 423 4530 ■ Break-
fast excl ■ www.back
packers.co.za ■ R
One of South Africa's
oldest backpacker hostels,
this place offers luxurious
rooms along with stan-
dard dorms. It has a very
experienced travel centre
that can help you with
your excursion plans.

Hermanus Backpackers
MAP U5 ■ 26 Flower St,
Hermanus ■ 028 312
4293 ■ R
This lively hostel has
dorms and self-contained
cottages. It offers activities
ranging from caged shark
dives at Gansbaai to cliff
walks, whale watching
and wine tasting along the
Walker Bay wine route.

Long Street Backpackers
MAP P5 ■ 209 Long St
■ 021 423 0615 ■ Breakfast
excl ■ www.longstreet
backpackers.com ■ R
The oldest and probably
the best backpacker
hostel along Long Street,
within easy reach of the
trendy nightspots. It's a
secure, friendly and lively
place for those who want
to be at the heart of the
urban action.

Otter's Bend Lodge
MAP F2 ■ Dassenberg Rd,
Franschhoek ■ 021 876
3200 ■ Breakfast excl
■ www.ottersbendlodge.
co.za ■ R
This budget hostel fills
a gap in Franschhoek's
accommodation scene,

and it's in a pretty location.
There's a dorm, three
en-suite rooms and two
cabins that sleep up to four
people. Otter's Bend Lodge
also arranges outdoor
activities for guests.

Sea Shack
MAP S2 ■ Cape Colum-
bine Nature Reserve,
Paternoster ■ 079 820
6824 ■ Breakfast excl
■ www.seashack.co.za
■ R
The ultimate backpacker
hostel for outdoor enthu-
siasts, Sea Shack offers
simple accommodation in
tents and wooden cabins.
Other attractions include
guided sea kayaking, boat
trips, snorkelling and
lovely walks through the
reserve and on the sandy
beaches. The power
provided is solar or gas.

St John's Waterfront Lodge
MAP P2 ■ 6 Braemar Rd,
Green Pt ■ 021 439 1404
■ Breakfast excl ■ www.
stjohns.co.za ■ R
Set in the suburb of Green
Point, this welcoming
and well-established
hostel offers rooms and
dorms and is a short
walk (not advisable late
at night) from the V&A
Waterfront and a bus
ride from the city.

Stumble Inn
MAP D2 ■ 12 Market St,
Stellenbosch ■ 021 887
4049 ■ Breakfast excl
■ www.stumbleinn
backpackers.co.za ■ R
Stumble Inn is located
close to historic Dorp
Street, and is thus very
convenient for exploring
the Stellenbosch CBD.
Facilities include a
swimming pool and
a TV lounge.

For a key to hotel price categories see p114

General Index

Acknowledgments

Author
Born in Britain and raised in Johannesburg, Philip Briggs is the author of more than a dozen travel guides about Africa. He is also a regular contributor to magazines such as *Travel Africa*, *Africa Geographic*, *Wanderlust* and *BBC Wildlife*

Additional contributor
Lucy Corne

Publishing Director Georgina Dee

Publisher Vivien Antwi

Design Director Phil Ormerod

Editorial Sophie Adam, Michelle Crane, Rachel Fox, Fay Franklin, Alison McGill, Sally Schafer, Hollie Teague, Ankita Awasthi Tröger

Cover Design Maxine Pedliham, Vinita Venugopal

Design Hansa Babra, Tessa Bindloss, Bharti Karakoti, Rahul Kumar, Bhavika Mathur, Ankita Sharma, Stuti Tiwari, Vinita Venugopal

Picture Research Subhadeep Biswas, Taiyaba Khatoon, Ellen Root, Rituraj Singh

Cartography Zafar ul Islam Khan, Suresh Kumar, James Macdonald, Casper Morris

DTP Jason Little

Production Luca Bazzoli

Factchecker Lizzie Williams

Proofreader Clare Peel

Indexer Helen Peters

First edition created by Quadrum Solutions, Mumbai

Revisions Parnika Bagla, Elspeth Beidas, Mohammad Hassan, Sumita Khatwani, Shikha Kulkarni, Chhavi Nagpal, Bandana Paul, Vagisha Pushp, Azeem Siddiqui, Beverly Smart, Hollie Teague, Priyanka Thakur, Stuti Tiwari, Lizzie Williams, Tanveer Zaidi

Rhapsode 29c; Merten Snijders 61cl, 67br, 68cla, 70bl; Ruby Soho 37tr; Tier Und Naturfotografie J und C Sohns 32cr; The Times / Shelley Christians 91br; Richard du Toit 79tr; David Wall Photo 72ca; Ariadne Van Zandbergen 12bl.

Gold Restaurant: JanTheron 58br.

Grande Provence Restaurant: 99cr.

Harbour House: 76br, 89clb.

iStockphoto.com: Agnieszka Gaul 3tr, 82–3, 106–7; Jan-Otto 49b; shumski 2tl, 8–9.

Karoo Classics: 94clb.

Kirstenbosch National Botanical Garden: 26tl, 27crb; *Bringing Condolences* by Norbert Shamyarira. 27tc.

La Motte: 37cl, 96tl.

La Parada: 77bc.

La Petite Colombe: Claire Gunn 58t.

Meerlust: 97crb.

Oranjezicht City Farm: Coco van Oppens 60tl.

Quagga Rare Books & Art: 88tr.

Rex Shutterstock: Gallo Images 62b.

Root 44 Market: 94ca.

Sevruga: 76tl.

Spier Wine Farm: 57cr, 61br.

Tokara: 95b, 98cla.

Woodstock Exchange: 72crb.

Cover

Front and spine: **Dreamstime.com: Bennymarty.**

Back: **4Corners:** Justin Foulkes tr; **AWL Images:** Michele Falzone crb; **Dreamstime.com:** Agaliza tl, Bennymarty b, Hongqi Zhang cla.

Pull Out Map Cover

Dreamstime.com: Bennymarty.

All other images © Dorling Kindersley

For further information see:
www.dkimages.com

DK | Penguin Random House

First edition 2008
Published in Great Britain by
Dorling Kindersley Limited
DK, One Embassy Gardens, 8 Viaduct Gardens, London SW11 7BW, UK

The authorised representative in the EEA is Dorling Kindersley Verlag GmbH. Arnulfstr. 124, 80636 Munich, Germany

Published in the United States by DK US, 1450 Broadway, Suite 801, New York, NY 10018, USA

Copyright © 2008, 2021 Dorling Kindersley Limited

A Penguin Random House Company

21 22 23 24 10 9 8 7 6 5 4 3 2 1

Reprinted with revisions 2010, 2014, 2017, 2019, 2021

ISSN 1479-344X
ISBN 978-0-2415-4434-1
Printed and bound in China

www.dk.com

As a guide to abbreviations in the visitor information blocks: **Adm** = *admission charge.*

Selected Street and Towns Index